To Joseph,

Be Amazing!

Sheryl Brown

THE
CONVENIENCE
REVOLUTION

BOOKS BY SHEP HYKEN

Moments of Magic: *Be a Star with Your Customers and Keep Them Forever*

The Loyal Customer: *A Lesson from a Cab Driver*

Only the Best on Success (coauthor)

Only the Best on Customer Service (coauthor)

Only the Best on Leadership (coauthor)

The Winning Spirit (coauthor)

Inspiring Others to Win (coauthor)

The Cult of the Customer: *Create an Amazing Experience That Turns Satisfied Customers into Customer Evangelists*

The Amazement Revolution: *Seven Customer Service Strategies to Create an Amazing Customer (and Employee) Experience*

Amaze Every Customer Every Time: *52 Tools for Delivering the Most Amazing Customer Service on the Planet*

Be Amazing or Go Home: *Seven Customer Service Habits That Create Confidence with Everyone*

The Convenience Revolution: *How to Deliver a Customer Service Experience That Disrupts the Competition and Creates Fierce Loyalty*

THE
CONVENIENCE
REVOLUTION

How to Deliver a Customer Service Experience

That Disrupts the Competition and

Creates Fierce Loyalty

SHEP HYKEN

Published and Distributed by
SOUND WISDOM
P.O. Box 310
Shippensburg, PA 17257-0310
717-530-2122
info@soundwisdom.com.
www.soundwisdom.com

Cover/Jacket designer Eileen Rockwell
Interior designed by Author Support

THE CONVENIENCE REVOLUTION:
How to Deliver a Customer Service Experience That Disrupts the Competition and Creates Fierce Loyalty

ISBN 13: 978-1-64095-052-8
ISBN 10: 1-64095-052-4
ISBN eBook: 978-1-64095-053-5

For Worldwide Distribution, Printed in the U.S.A.
1 2 3 4 5 6 7 8 / 21 20 19 18

First Edition

CONTENTS

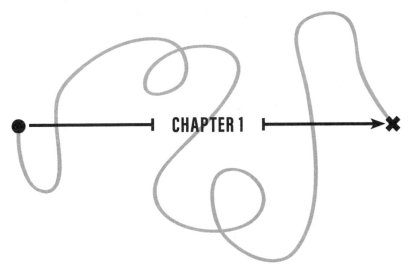

CHAPTER 1

How to Use This Book

This book is built around six big ideas that, together, form an ongoing, unstoppable shift in the relationship between buyers and sellers. I call this shift the Convenience Revolution, and I believe any organization that ignores it is, at best, missing an opportunity to provide their customers with a better experience; at worst, they're risking disruption by a competitor.

Here you'll find in-depth examinations of the six Convenience Principles that drive this revolution, including plenty of real-life examples from the companies leading it. My aim in sharing their stories is to entertain you, intrigue you, and get you thinking about how each of these six big ideas can impact your world. By the end of the book, I want to leave you with at least one big idea of your own, an idea you can apply to your own business in a way that more than compensates for the money, time and attention you've invested here. That's my deliverable.

Even though not every concept I share will be relevant to every business, I still want to suggest that you read the book from beginning to end, without skipping any of the sections. Doing so will instill a deeper understanding of the foundational concept of convenience, and make it easier for you to identify the takeaways and action items that will give you an edge over your competition.

Speaking of takeaways: At the end of each Convenience Principle, you'll find a special section called *The Takeaways*. This section is extremely important, and I urge you not just to read it, but to write down your answers to the questions you find there. By taking just a few minutes to jot down your responses, you can apply what you learned to your own world, set new priorities for yourself and your organization, and identify the best opportunities to raise the convenience bar in a way that delivers a lasting competitive advantage.

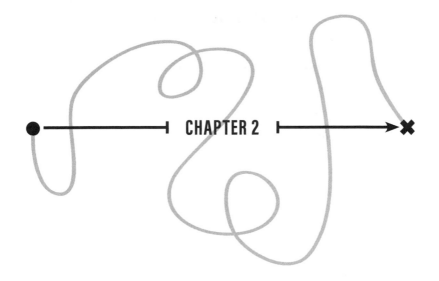

The Convenience Revolution: An Overview

Whether you've heard about it or not, whether you believe in it or not, whether you're ready for it or not, the Convenience Revolution is well under way, and your customers are enthusiastically embracing it. The only real question is whether it will disrupt you ... or if you will use it to disrupt your competitors – or maybe even your entire industry. If you're ready to set off a seismic shift in your company's customer experience, then this book is for you.

The Oxford Handbook of the History of Consumption explains that it is "the relentless pursuit of convenience" that determines "the temporal texture of individual lives, and the pulse of society as a whole."[1] That's another way of saying that today's ever-accelerating customer demand for convenience will continue to disrupt and even wipe out old, unresponsive industries, create brand-new ones and transform those that adapt quickly enough to survive. This will happen with exponentially greater speed as time passes. There are six specific ways in which today's business leaders can prepare (you'll start reading about them in the next chapter), and my urgent advice is that you learn about and adopt them before your competition does.

CONVENIENCE QUESTION

- **How easy is it to do business with you?**

ANCIENT ROOTS

I've been speaking, writing and posting videos about the Convenience Revolution for some time now. One of the questions I often hear is: "When did the Convenience Revolution begin?"

It's a great question, and over the years I've done a lot of digging to track down the best possible answer, which appears to be 534 A.D.

That's the year the Eastern Roman Emperor Justinian formalized *Codex Justinianus*, also known as the Justinian Code, a comprehensive set of laws that would serve as the legal foundation of Western civilization for centuries to come. One of

---

1   https://books.google.ie/books?id=bnvQDIeIsAUC&pg=PT324&lpg=PT324&dq="understanding+the +relentless+pursuit+of+convenience+is,+in+part,+a+matter+of"

its fascinating provisions is a decree that each major crossroad of the Byzantine Empire would feature a store "to enable the people to buy the daily necessities of life." As far as anyone can tell, that's the first evidence of the Convenience Revolution ... and for what it's worth, the first recorded launch of a convenience store chain.

The key word here, of course, is "convenience." Back in ancient times, crossroads were much further apart than, say, the distance between two Starbucks on the same city block in midtown Manhattan. Justinian recognized that there needed to be provisions available for the convenience of people traveling vast distances. Presumably, he was responding to what we call "consumer demand" today.

The Convenience Revolution has deep, ancient roots, but the desire to make things more convenient for people is more relevant today than ever. I like to think of *Codex Justinianus* as an undersea earthquake that triggered the first ripples of a wave that started back in 534 A.D. – or who knows, maybe even earlier. Ever since, that wave has grown into a uniquely disruptive force, a tidal wave of customer convenience. And you have a choice: You can either ride that wave or be swept away by it.

MODERN IMPACT

You can trace that wave's trajectory from Emperor Justinian to Jefferson "Uncle Johnny" Green, nearly 14 centuries later. In 1927, Uncle Johnny came up with an idea to better serve the customers of the Southland Ice Company, where he worked. He shared his idea with the boss, and his boss loved it and told him to give it a try. To understand the power of Uncle

Johnny's idea, and its connection to Justinian, you need to understand what the Southland Ice Company did for its customers up to this point: it sold them ice.

Remember, this was before refrigerators took over American homes. Back in 1927, to keep your food cold, you put it in an icebox, a literal box that held a big block of ice in a special compartment at the bottom. When the ice melted, you bought another huge block of ice. The Southland Ice Company had 21 locations in Texas where people went to pick up huge chunks of ice.

CONVENIENCE INSIGHT

Make the customer's day a little easier.

Uncle Johnny had the crazy idea of keeping bread, milk, eggs and other perishable products on top of the ice in the store and offering them for sale. That way, when customers came in to buy ice, they'd also have the chance to make additional purchases. He focused on basic necessities, the kinds of products people bought to save a trip to a bigger store. They'd pay a little more than they would at a typical grocery store, but they'd save themselves a little time and trouble, and make their day a little easier.

Uncle Johnny's idea is now a standard business model,

leveraging convenience and charging a little more. There are other models, which we'll examine later in the book.

Long story short: The Southland Ice Company's revenues exploded. Uncle Johnny took Justinian's idea – "to enable the people to buy the daily necessities of life" – and repurposed it for the modern age. Before long, Southland was no longer an ice company; it became a convenience company. The newly established Southland Corporation eventually rebranded its chain of ice block outlets with a snappier, more powerful name: "7-Eleven" – to reflect the (then unheard-of) practice of opening at 7 a.m. and closing at 11 p.m. Notice again, the emphasis on making things more convenient for the customer. Of course, nowadays there are more than 64,000 7-Eleven stores, and they're the dominant player in a highly competitive sector of the economy.

7-Eleven, and all modern convenience stores, are following Justinian's innovation: providing only the items you need on your journey. They offer the items you most want and need so you can get in and out quickly, just like Justinian had in mind. Customers wanted that kind of convenience in 524 A.D., they wanted it in 1927, and they want it today.

Recall the critical choice Uncle Johnny made: to ride the wave of consumer demand for convenience, rather than wait for it to flatten him. He didn't ignore that wave, or pretend it didn't exist or wasn't relevant to his business. He challenged his own organization's status quo and stepped outside the prevailing comfort zone ... to "enable the people to buy the daily necessities of life." He made the right choice.

If you doubt any of that, I'd like to pose two questions:

1. When was the last time you visited a store to pick up a big block of ice to put into your icebox?
2. When was the last time you visited a convenience store?

I rest my case. That wave Uncle Johnny rode to economic success has only picked up speed and strength since 1927. It's now a tsunami. And as it moves forward, it will continue to impact everyone and everything in its path, including your business.

Convenience is relevant to your business, no matter what your business happens to be, and no matter whether your goal is to serve businesses, consumers or some combination of the two. It would be a strategic catastrophe to assume you are already "convenient enough" for your customer, and it's a potentially huge marketplace advantage to make what you offer to the customer a little more convenient.

CONVENIENCE INSIGHT

Somewhere right now, there's a hotel guest who knows there's a soda machine down the hall selling a can of Coke for $1.50 ... but who's choosing the $4.50 can of Coke from the minibar anyway.

ARE YOU RIDING THE WAVE?

Here's the thing we must bear in mind: once customers experience convenience, they tend to expect more of it ... and they tend to spend their money based on where they feel they are most likely to get it.

That means, if we want to ride the ever-intensifying wave like Uncle Johnny did, we need to be willing to listen to customers about what is and isn't convenient in their world ... and even anticipate what they're going to consider convenient tomorrow.

If you're wondering what the desire for convenience might look like as it approaches you, I invite you to consider the possibility that it might come in the form of a suggestion from one of your customers. Whether you choose to listen to that suggestion or not might make the difference between you and your business riding the wave of disruption ... or drowning beneath it.

CONVENIENCE QUESTION

- **Who could possibly do a better job of telling you what's convenient, and what isn't, than your customer?**

Warren Danziger, who subscribes to my online newsletter, *The Shepard Letter,* shared this true story with me. It was time for Warren to call the HVAC company he had used for years to come out for the semiannual inspection of his air conditioner and furnace. As usual, Warren received excellent service. Shortly after the service call, he received an email requesting that he complete a survey, which he was happy to do. Upon completion of the survey, he was sent a $15 coupon to print out, which he was supposed to provide to the company at the time of his next service call.

Warren replied to that offer in a way that perfectly captures the essence of the Convenience Revolution. It read as follows:

> *Thank you for the coupon. Why is the onus on me to save the coupon for 6 months and to remember to present it to the repair person? If you really mean it, make a note in your computer file and automatically deduct it from my next service call.*

Warren recognized a "friction point" that the company may or may not have been aware of (you're going to be hearing that word "friction" a lot, by the way). The company that listens to and acts on this kind of customer feedback – or better yet, anticipates it – is the company that will position itself to ride the swelling wave of consumer demand for convenience ... and establish a powerful marketplace advantage. On the other side of the equation, the company that gets this kind of email and ignores it, or dismisses it as "not the way we do things," is asking for trouble in the current market environment.

Now, there may be some cynical people who say the company purposely makes the customer hold onto the coupon for six months, assuming he or she will forget about it or lose it and it won't be redeemed. However, I don't think that was this company's intent; I think they just wanted to show some generosity and appreciation. Warren recognized there was a better way to do it, and he started a conversation. Unfortunately, the company chose not to continue that conversation ... which, in today's world, amounts to a white flag of surrender.

Sadly, his suggestion went unheeded. The door was left open for a competitor. Has that ever happened in your organization?

CONVENIENCE INSIGHT

Every time a customer shares feedback with you, consider it an opportunity to create a disruptive market advantage over your competition.

I suspect the reason the company didn't continue the conversation was it had grown used to doing business in a certain way. That's basically asking for someone else to disrupt your market.

What the leaders at the HVAC company could have done with Warren's suggestion was listen ... and seriously consider changing their approach. There are any number of ways they could have put his good idea into practice. For instance, they could have sent the coupon with something like the following explanation:

You are welcome to print out the coupon as a reminder to schedule your next appointment, or don't print it and save a tree. Either way, we'll remember to apply it to the next service call. Thank you again for your business!

All too often, companies think they are doing right by the customer, when in reality, they are adding friction. To survive and thrive, we need to listen to our customers ... and anticipate what's likely to reduce friction in their world. In other words, we need to ask ourselves, "What would Uncle Johnny do to make the customer's day a little easier?" This book is here to help you follow his example by analyzing what's really going on in the customer's world.

CONVENIENCE QUESTIONS:

- **What friction already exists in your customer's world?**
- **What friction can you remove, or at least reduce?**
- **What friction could you be adding without realizing it?**
- **What are the best ways to minimize or reduce that inconvenience?**
- **What could you do today to make it just a little easier to do business with you and your company?**
- **How can you make your customer's day a little easier?**
- **What are your competitors doing to reduce friction?**
- **How can you be even more convenient than your competitors?**

These are the kinds of questions we will be exploring together in this book. In today's environment, the customer expects not only good service, but also a better, more convenient experience. So, making it easier for people to do business with us has now become not just an option, but a strategic imperative ... and a critical differentiator in every marketplace.

There are six ways you can use convenience to disrupt your competition, and you'll learn about them in the next chapter.

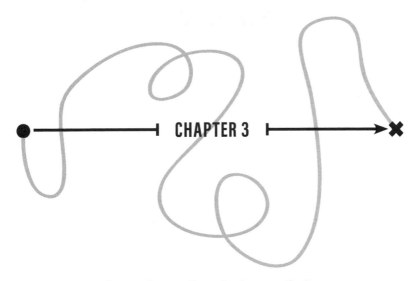

CHAPTER 3

The Six Principles of the Convenience Revolution

Note: *Throughout this book I use the word "customer" as an umbrella term, even though in your world you may call your customer a guest, a member, a client, a patient, a resident or some other name.*

In this chapter, I'll introduce the core concepts of the book, although we'll go into much greater depth and detail in the chapters that follow. For now, the six principles of the Convenience Revolution – by which you will either disrupt the market or be disrupted – are as follows:

#1: REDUCING FRICTION

Make doing business with you as easy as possible, taking down as many barriers as possible to buying or using a product or service.

Reducing friction means anticipating and removing any barriers that stand between the customer and the product or service experience. This principle leads the list because it is the essence of convenience, and serves as the foundation for the five principles that follow.

Every company profiled in this book embraces this principle to some extent, but companies featured in the "Reducing Friction" chapter have built their brand's promise around breaking down barriers for their customers. These companies make Reducing Friction a critical component of their business strategy, giving them a competitive advantage and, in some cases, taking it to the point of disrupting and transforming their entire industry.

CONVENIENCE INSIGHT

———

Friction is a hassle in your customer's world. Anything that removes friction, regardless of the source, is likely to improve your relationship with the customer.

#2: SELF-SERVICE

Let your customers control the transaction/interaction.

Self-service is the wave of the future. In air travel, retail, banking, hospitality and countless other sectors of the economy, self-service is transforming the way customers buy and use products and services.

Not all self-service options increase convenience when they are implemented, and not all consumers embrace self-service options that companies offer. As a recent study by Sheryl Kimes and Joe Collier in the *MIT Sloan Management Review* highlighted, "Managers significantly underestimated the need for employee interaction during a self-service experience, especially when customers were exhibiting technology anxiety. Customers want a safety net in case a failure occurs, we found, and they explicitly want an employee to be available."[1]

CONVENIENCE INSIGHT

A self-service option may improve your customer's experience with your company ... but not all self-service options do.

In this chapter, I profile companies that have taken this advice to heart and created innovative, well-designed

1　http://sloanreview.mit.edu/article/how-customers-view-self-service-technologies/

self-service options with a human fallback. These are state-of-the-art, 21st century interaction strategies that give customers control over the process, save them time and keep them coming back for more.

#3. TECHNOLOGY

Create new processes, tools and ways of interacting that make life easier for customers.

According to linguists, the word "technology" comes from an ancient Greek phrase, *tekno logia*, meaning "systematic treatment of an art, craft or technique."[2] That's still a pretty good way of defining technology: a systematic treatment, or process, that makes accomplishing a goal easier. If it's a treatment we haven't seen or used before, we usually call it an invention or a breakthrough.

Today's customers have come to expect a steady stream of technological breakthroughs ... which means they expect rising levels of convenience from the tools they use. Consider how a single smartphone has not tens, not hundreds, not thousands, but millions of times more computing power than NASA had at its disposal when it sent a team of astronauts to the moon and brought them home safely back in 1969! And, each new generation of communication and computing devices seems to consistently raise the bar higher still.

It's no surprise, then, that customers are always on the lookout for relationships with companies that will provide

---

2   https://books.google.com/books?id=AYZFBAAAQBAJ&lpg=PA443&ots=FSa-LdzU6C&dq=Greek%20phrase%20tekno%20logia%20systematic%20learning&pg=PA443#v=onepage&q&f=false

newer, more exciting, and more efficient ways for them to leverage the astonishing technological power at their disposal. In the Technology chapter, we look at some of the companies that are committed to delivering these bar-raising breakthroughs. Most of what you will find in this section couldn't have been predicted five years ago. By extension, most of what will happen in the next five years can't be predicted here. But what we can do is look at the trajectory now being established by some of the most dynamic market leaders, as well as the technological trends most likely to shape the Convenience Revolution in the days, months and years ahead.

CONVENIENCE INSIGHT

Customers appreciate a systematic process that makes life easier. If your technology does that, they will return to you again and again.

#4: SUBSCRIPTION

Establish automated, scheduled delivery of products and services that people use on a regular basis.

The subscription business model is a growth strategy with a popularity that seems unlikely to recede anytime soon. Pioneered by newspapers, magazines and book clubs, subscriptions have now expanded into many other sectors of the economy. As *Entrepreneur* magazine noted in March 2015,

"The subscription model owes its success to the optimal balance of value it provides to both the company and the customer. For customers, the value lies in the convenience. First, there's the autopilot simplicity of subscriptions that removes the thinking out of a purchase decision. Subscribers never have to remember to reorder every month, which gives them the reassurance that they will have whatever they need before they actually need it. ... Second, subscriptions offer a flat rate which helps customers stay within their budget – always."[3]

From the company's point of view, what's better than a repeat purchase? A repeat purchase that the customer makes automatically, month after month! The old adage about it being far more economical to retain a current customer than it is to secure a new one takes on a powerful new relevance in the Convenience Revolution. In the Subscription chapter, I profile companies that have turned this age-old business strategy into a powerful information-age market advantage ... one that has the potential to disrupt and transform entire industries (just ask Blockbuster Video!).

CONVENIENCE INSIGHT

———

A subscription model sets your customer's purchase preferences on autopilot.

---

3   https://www.entrepreneur.com/article/243573

#5: DELIVERY

Bring the product to the customer, rather than making the customer go to the product.

As this book is being written, the restaurant industry is in the process of undergoing a major transformation. According to a recent National Restaurant Association forecast, 56 percent of all adults surveyed said they would order delivery from a table-service restaurant, if available.[4] This is a huge shift in buying preferences, and as a result, many restaurants that have never offered a delivery option before are offering one now.

What's happening in the world of restaurants is just the tip of the iceberg. Making one less trip to the store (whatever kind of store that may be) is often perceived as a major lifestyle advantage for today's busy customers. This aspect of the Convenience Revolution reflects a rapidly-accelerating expectation from customers: you bring it to me. There have been significant changes in both communications technology and consumer thinking in the past decade, and today's buyer is far more likely than previous generations to place an order for delivery, and far less likely to quibble about the extra charge for doing so. This means there is the potential for a higher-margin transaction ... and a higher lifetime customer value. In the Delivery chapter, you'll learn about companies that have picked up on this trend and are building it into their business plan ... or even making it the heart of their business plan!

Convenience Insight: Customers like it when the product or service comes to them, because they don't have to go anywhere.

---

4   http://www.restaurant.org/News-Research/News/State-of-the-industry-We-are-living-in-a-millennia

#6: ACCESS

Decide where your market is ... and then make sure you're there.

What happens if your customer wants your product or service at 2:00 in the morning? What happens if your customer doesn't feel like driving all the way across town? What if there's an off-hour emergency? We'll take a closer look at some leading-edge companies that have found innovative answers to these and similar questions by dramatically easing the access to their people, products and services.

That ease of access might come in the form of flexible or expanded hours, but it might also come in the form of newer, more customer-friendly ways of delivering the product or service, or in the form of what I call strategic pervasiveness: the familiar experience of seeing a certain company logo show up over and over again, no matter where you go. For example, how far do you have to drive before you spot a Starbucks? In my world, it's just a few minutes in any direction!

Once upon a time, the best example of cutting-edge access was the 24-hour convenience store. Today, the whole question of customer access has been transformed by the relentless rise of near-infinite options in online retail. Customer expectations of access are rising just as steadily. The companies you'll read about in the Access chapter have found ways to create a competitive advantage by staying ahead of the curve of customer access expectations.

So, those are the six principles driving the new economy in which we all now live and operate. You don't have to compete in all six – unless you want to – but if you can't find one or

CONVENIENCE INSIGHT

Access means raising the bar for customers when it comes to availability, communication and/or location.

two areas where your organization can raise its game, prepare to be disrupted!

Before we move on, let me pose a question that I've now asked countless participants in my speeches and training programs:

Given what you now know about CONVENIENCE ... about how customers are moving toward options that REDUCE FRICTION, offer SELF-SERVICE, make SUBSCRIPTION easy, leverage breakthroughs in TECHNOLOGY, provide DELIVERY, and give greater levels of ACCESS ...

What would you say is the most convenient company in the world to do business with?

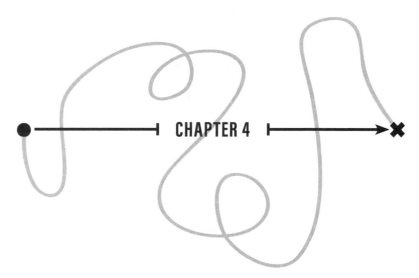

CHAPTER 4

Amazon: The Most Convenient Company on Earth

"If you're competitor-focused, you have to wait until there is a competitor doing something. Being customer-focused allows you to be more pioneering."[1]

– JEFF BEZOS, CHIEF EXECUTIVE OFFICER, AMAZON

I f you're like most people I talk to, one name instantly springs to mind when asked to identify the single most convenient company that they've ever done business with: Amazon.

---

1 https://www.usnews.com/news/best-leaders/articles/2008/11/19/americas-best-leaders-jeff-bezos-amazoncom-ceo

Let's look at just how far this company has come in what is, by historical standards, a very brief period of time.

Amazon.com was founded in 1994. If you remember the release of the film *Jurassic Park*, (1993) you remember a time when people who wanted to buy something couldn't just go online and "check Amazon" ... because Amazon didn't exist yet!

The online pioneer started out proclaiming itself as "Earth's biggest bookstore" ... but as we all know now, it quickly moved beyond that descriptor to offer "Earth's biggest selection" of virtually anything that can be shipped to consumers. Today, you can buy lettuce, perfume, stockings, fine art, a $10,000 acoustic guitar and just about everything in between by logging in to your Amazon account. By the way, if you live in the United States and your household doesn't have an Amazon account, you are in the minority!

That transition – from Amazon being "how you buy books" to Amazon being "how you buy just about anything" – may be the biggest business story of our time. It will continue to be the big story for at least the next decade. Why do I say that? Because in the years since Amazon's founding, it is not so much the Internet, but this one company that has transformed the world of retailing. And in a very real sense, whether we operate in the retail sector or not, and whether we realize it or not, we are all competing with Amazon.

CONVENIENCE QUESTIONS:

HOW HAS THE EXPERIENCE OF BUYING FROM AMAZON AFFECTED YOUR CUSTOMERS' EXPECTATIONS ABOUT YOUR ABILITY TO ...

- ... REDUCE FRICTION?
- ... PROVIDE A USER-FRIENDLY, SELF-SERVICE OPTION?
- ... LEVERAGE THE LATEST TECHNOLOGY TO MAKE THEIR LIVES A LITTLE EASIER?
- ... SAVE TIME ON REPEAT PURCHASES THROUGH SUBSCRIPTION SERVICES?
- ... PROVIDE QUICK, AFFORDABLE DELIVERY?
- ... BE THERE FOR THEM WHEN THEY NEED YOU, OR EVEN WHEN THEY JUST FEEL LIKE BROWSING?

The fact that we are all competing with Amazon is neither good nor bad – it's just a fact; it's the reality we all face. I believe we should all be asking ourselves:

What happened to make this the reality that all business leaders now face, and how did it happen?

First off, let's consider the dimensions of what happened, because it can be a little difficult to get our heads around. Amazon is so pervasive now that we run the risk of taking it for granted, of thinking of it as an essential reality, like air or water, something that has always been there. But Amazon is a *real* business with a *real* growth curve based on *real* strategies that have delivered measurable results with which we should be familiar. Take a moment to closely consider the following significant figures.

AMAZON BY THE NUMBERS

- **394** – E-commerce, which was literally impossible to measure in the early 1990s because no one was buying anything online, accounted for over $394 billion in 2016 in the U.S. alone – roughly 8 percent of all retail sales, and rising sharply each year. That's thanks in large measure to Amazon's explosive growth in the sector.

- **43** – The current estimate is that Amazon accounts for 43 percent of all U.S. online retail sales; the figure is projected to expand to 50 percent over the next four years.

- **7.5** – Approximately 7.5 percent of Seattle's working-age population works for Amazon.[2] That's a staggering figure. *Inc.* magazine has called Seattle "America's largest company town."

- **300** – There are roughly 300 million active Amazon accounts worldwide.[3]

- **77** – One generous estimate claims that 77 percent of U.S. households are enrolled in Amazon Prime, while more modest estimates put the number at 54 percent.[4][5] The company's subscription service includes streaming video access, free two-day delivery and other benefits. That means between half and three-quarters of American households are enrolled in Amazon's high-margin premium program. That's an astonishing achievement.

- **8** – Eight out of 10 Amazon customers buy something from Amazon at least once a month.[6]

- **470** – In terms of market capitalization (the share

2   https://www.inc.com/business-insider/facts-about-amazon-jeff-bezos-seattle-2017.html
3   http://uk.businessinsider.com/how-amazons-payments-service-could-solve-its-biggest-weakness-against-paypal-2017-2?r=US&IR=T
4   https://files.constantcontact.com/150f9af2201/d8e982eb-fcc7-41b4-bd58-eba64185962d.pdf
5   https://cowen.bluematrix.com/sellside/EmailDocViewer?mime=pdf&co=Cowen&id=agriswold@qz.com&source=mail&encrypt=aedf2c61-81f3-41b0-8b6a-727a7dc48b28
6   https://expandedramblings.com/index.php/amazon-statistics/

price multiplied by the number of shares outstanding), Amazon is easily the most valuable retailer in America with a market value in excess of $470 billion, as of this writing. That makes it more valuable than all publicly traded brick-and-mortar retailers *combined*. Read that last sentence again. Yes, I double-checked it. Amazon is worth more than Walmart, Target, Best Buy, JC Penney and all other publicly-traded retailers combined.[7]

This brief overview gives you some sense of the economic revolution that Amazon has been leading since 1994. It's huge. And with that information, we can move forward with our second question: How in the world did Amazon do this?

The answer is simpler than a lot of people expect: Amazon committed itself to delivering a convenient customer experience – specifically, the six Convenience Principles shared in the previous chapter.

This is the open secret that made Amazon's other operations so successful. Over the years, Amazon made sure it set and maintained the "gold standard" in all six of the Convenience Principles. Not only that, Amazon committed itself to reshaping customer expectations about what is and isn't convenient. It's continually raising the bar in the areas of Reducing Friction, Self-Service, Subscription, Delivery, Access, and Technology. It has continually invested in improving those six areas, and the investments are paying off.

"In the old world, you devoted 30 percent of your time

---

7   http://uk.businessinsider.com/the-extraordinary-size-of-amazon-in-one-chart-2017-1?r=US&IR=T

to building a great service and 70 percent of your time
to shouting about it. In the new world, that inverts."

— JEFF BEZOS

For examples of how the company has established and maintained its leading edge in each of these six areas, read on.

AMAZON'S SIX CONVENIENCE REVOLUTIONS

Reducing Friction. Self-Service. Technology. Subscription. Delivery. Access. Amazon is a disruptive, revolutionary force and world-class leader, in all six of these convenience areas. In this chapter, we take a closer look at each of these revolutions. By the way, the examples shared in this chapter, while impressive, are not meant to be a complete list of the innovative ways that Amazon delivers convenience to its customers. That would be virtually impossible, since Amazon is always developing new ideas and adapting older ones to give the customer the best possible experience. However, the concepts I'll be sharing with you here will be more than enough to make the point: that Amazon may well be the single most convenient company on the planet.

#1: Reducing Friction

Making the purchasing process as easy as possible; taking down as many barriers as possible to buying or using a product or service.

If you spend just a little time examining your own relationship with Amazon, you'll probably realize that reducing friction, and keeping the customer experience hassle-free, is the uniting principle behind its whole, mind-bogglingly huge suite of offerings. Consider, for instance, what most of us have come to take for granted when buying from Amazon: easy returns.

Amazon prides itself on a hassle-free return policy and, by the time you read these words, it will have rolled out that policy so that it applies to every single order you place through Amazon – including orders from third-party sellers (retailers that aren't Amazon, but use its platform).

As you've already read, close to two out of three American households are enrolled in Amazon Prime, which offers members a wide range of benefits, including free two-day shipping. That's friction-free, no-hassle shopping at its best, right? Well ... yes and no. As it has made a habit of doing throughout its history, Amazon has raised the bar. Free shipping in two days or less was so popular that Amazon has now set up a network of distribution centers in specific cities that offer Amazon Prime members free shipping in two hours or less for certain items.[8]

Think about that – I don't know about you, but most of the people I talk to tell me that free shipping within two hours scores pretty high on the reducing-the-hassle-factor scale. Notice what happened when Amazon made that available: the expectation bar got raised, not only for Amazon Prime members, but for everyone else those Amazon Prime members buy from! Even if you never even expected that kind of rapid delivery before ... you expect it now![9]

Another classic example of reducing friction is Amazon's patented "1-Click" ordering, which lets you connect a credit,

---

8   http://uk.businessinsider.com/amazon-prime-now-how-it-works-2017-6?r=US&IR=T
9   By the way, you may have noticed that the accelerated delivery Amazon offers could easily have been placed in the Delivery category. That's one of the key points to remember about the Reducing Friction principle. It's the foundation of all the other categories, and as a result there are often overlaps.

debit or Amazon Store Card and address you ship to, so you can place orders with the single click of a button. You can also quickly change your information if necessary. How friction-free is that? So much so that other brands followed up with their versions of "1-Click" ordering. Visa developed a one-click technology called "Visa Checkout" and PayPal created "One Touch," while Barnes & Noble has "Instant Purchase."

There are countless examples of innovative ways Amazon reduces the hassle factor for its customers. These few examples, though, give you an idea of the extraordinary power of this transformative idea, which is the bedrock principle of the Convenience Revolution.

#2: Self-Service

Letting customers control the transaction/interaction.

Everything you do on Amazon, from researching individual purchases to comparing prices, from making your final selection to checking out, is done at your pace, and with your priorities driving the process. There are no high-pressure sales tactics. In fact, there's barely any pressure at all, beyond reminding you about what's in your cart and letting you know what other people with similar interests have purchased or examined. Everything you do has Frequently Asked Questions that you can reference at any time, and it's incredibly easy to complete your purchase without talking to a person.

What's on the horizon? Amazon is currently testing a grocery store in Seattle that uses "computer vision and deep learning technologies" to figure out what you've put in your basket, so it can charge you automatically as you walk out the door. No checkout lines! Amazon explains: "Our Just Walk Out Technology automatically detects when products are taken from or returned to the shelves and keeps track of them in a virtual cart. When you're done shopping, you can just leave the store. Shortly after, we'll charge your Amazon account and send you a receipt." They're still working out the kinks, but the concept has the potential to transform the shopping experience.

#3. Technology

Creating new processes, tools and ways of interacting that make life easier for customers.

Let's start with the most obvious example: the Amazon website itself is a constantly updated, cutting-edge example of intuitive, ergonomically-tested, multiple-industry-transforming technology. Consumer tech product breakthroughs include the game-changing Kindle and Kindle Fire e-readers, and the equally game-changing Echo Dot and Alexa smart speakers. These leverage the power of artificial intelligence, allowing users to issue spoken commands to play music, turn on the TV, read an audiobook, order groceries, check the weather and carry out hundreds of other tasks you might never have imagined a speaker could do ... unless you happened to be Jeff Bezos, Amazon's CEO.

Another popular innovation is the Dash button, which lets you order everything from soap to printer ink cartridges to food items and more. For example, you can have a Dash button on the side of your washing machine. When you see you're getting low on detergent, you just push the button and your order is placed. Similar to 1-Click ordering, once you connect a method of payment with your address, you literally order an item with the touch of a button. It doesn't get more convenient than that!

Not surprisingly, the company also offers its cutting-edge Amazon Web Service (AWS) cloud computing solutions to enterprise clients, as well as small- and mid-sized businesses. In short, it's a major player in this arena, at all levels, and likely to remain one. Much more is on the drawing board. We just don't know what it is yet.

The truly remarkable thing about this category, though, is that Bezos didn't invent most of the technologies that have made his company's global dominance possible. He didn't invent online retailing, nor did he invent the e-reader. He didn't invent streaming video or voice recognition software. He didn't invent any of the core technologies his company uses today to deliver the world's most convenient customer experience. What he did do, though, was notice the ways that technology could be used to consistently exceed customer expectations in each of the six Convenience Principles ... and then adapted the existing technology toward that end.

In doing so, Bezos really has created a world in which all of us, whether we realize it or not, are competing with Amazon. He's raised the bar for all businesses.

#4: Subscription

Automatically delivering products and services that people use on a regular basis.

Amazon's Subscribe and Save option allows customers to set up regularly scheduled deliveries of repeat purchases. They can also get extra savings by subscribing to five or more products at one address on a fixed monthly delivery date. Batteries, diapers, toothpaste, pet food, you name it – Amazon has found an easy way for you to set up a subscription plan to have it delivered on a regular basis, determined by you.

Talk about making your day a little easier! Imagine that 25-pound bag of dog food showing up at your doorstep, saving you the hassle of going to the store, loading it into your shopping cart, hoisting it onto the checkout belt to be scanned, packing it into your car, driving it home, and lugging it to your front door! You save time, gas and (given Amazon's aggressive pricing strategy) money.

By the way, Amazon Prime itself is a highly popular subscription service offering that includes, among other things, tons of popular and original streaming video content.

#5: Delivery

Bringing the product to the customer, rather than making the customer go to the product.

Amazon's business model is built around the idea of convenient delivery of goods to customers. Indeed, prompt, trackable delivery is part of the company's brand promise. The familiar Amazon package, including the little "smile arrow" pointing from A to Z, has become iconic – and even a kind of shorthand for "I'm having a good day now." (One online review I found read: "Feeling spoiled – just got home to two big Amazon boxes.")

You've already read about the astonishing two-hour delivery time that some Amazon Prime members enjoy. What does the future hold? Hard to say, but you can expect it to be big. *USA*

Today reported not long ago that the company is "quietly building out what analysts say looks like its own delivery company, one that could ultimately bypass UPS and FedEx."[10]

In the meantime, the company is constantly innovating its delivery options, including recently announced plans to "safely get packages to customers in 30 minutes or less using unmanned aerial vehicles, also called drones." The drone plan, as this book goes to press, is in development as part of Amazon Prime Air, which serves as an air cargo delivery service with 32 aircraft, based out of Hebron, Kentucky.

#6: Access

Deciding where your market is ... and then making sure you're there.

Amazon is the ultimate 24/7 retailer. You can shop there at 2:00 in the afternoon or 2:00 in the morning, dressed in your PJs or in a suit and tie. It's up to you. A typical online review reads, "Maybe I'm weird but Amazon has never given me any reason to complain. I've been a customer since 2005 and have yet to have a bad transaction. I did have an order that seemed to take forever to arrive, but when I checked on it, it was coming from South Korea. Since then I've paid attention to where the Amazon partner is located." The company's service, overwhelmingly virtual rather than voice to voice, wins consistently high marks. Even though most queries are resolved remotely, customers don't seem to mind waiting for an email reply. And if they do mind, there is a phone number to call. Connecting with an Amazon

---

10 https://www.usatoday.com/story/tech/news/2016/01/12/amazon-shipping-france-colis-priv/78686016/

customer support representative typically validates that the customer made the right decision to do business with Amazon.

The company is moving aggressively into the world of brick-and-mortar retailing, a major strategic initiative that will expand its access points for its customers even further. The company recently completed the acquisition of supermarket chain Whole Foods, giving Amazon a massive new platform for connecting with customers in person. As you might have expected, Amazon Prime members get a discount when they shop at a physical Whole Foods location, thereby connecting the two shopping experiences and broadening access even further by encouraging online orders.

Recently, Amazon Go, a self-service grocery store, opened in Seattle; there are also a dozen physical Amazon bookstores located in strategic urban locations in the U.S., with more on the way. Add it all up, and you've got a company that's committed to engaging with customers wherever they are, and whenever they want to connect.

In this overview of Amazon Books – its chain of physical bookstores – Amazon shows us all what 21st century access looks and feels like:

> *As a physical extension of Amazon.com, Amazon Books integrates the benefits of offline and online shopping to help you find books and devices you'll love. ... Amazon Books is a store without walls – there are thousands of books available in store and millions more available at Amazon.com. Walk out of the store with a book or device; lighten your load and buy it online (Prime customers, of course, won't pay for shipping);*

download a book for your Kindle; or add a product to your Amazon Wish List, so someone else can buy it.[11]

Before we move on, it's worth noting that Amazon has consistently chosen to reinvest its earnings into processes and platforms that reduce friction for customers ... and it has just as consistently chosen a low-margin model that keeps prices competitive for its massive, loyal customer base. That's the combination I want you to notice: investment in convenience, along with a price that is, although not always the lowest, reliably among the lowest.

Of course, those aren't the only two strategic choices to be made in support of a business model that embraces what I'm calling the Convenience Revolution. But I'd be remiss in my duty if I didn't point out how consistently Amazon has pursued these two strategies ... and how astonishingly strong the marketplace response has been.

"Your margin is my opportunity."

– JEFF BEZOS

Since its founding, Amazon has issued a powerful challenge to the rest of the business world: to build intense customer loyalty through a relentless, all-consuming, never-ending focus on expanding convenience for the customer. In the pages that follow, you'll find true stories of many innovative companies, large and small, that have taken on Amazon's challenge. You can take on that challenge, too.

---

11   https://www.amazon.com/b?node=13270229011

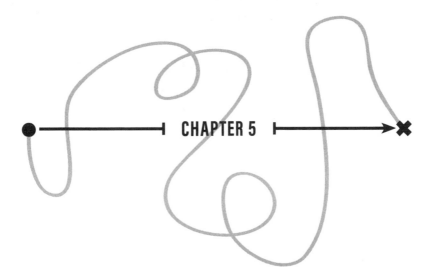

CHAPTER 5

An In-Depth Look at Principle One: Reduce Friction

"Friction is the enemy of customer experience. It frustrates the customer, annoys your team and stops business growth. And, if friction remains within the buyer's journey, it can stop future sales."[1]

– SHAYLA PRICE

I've called the irreversible marketplace shift toward convenience a revolution, one that can be broken down into six powerful guiding principles. It's time now for a deeper exploration of the first principle, the one critical idea that both encompasses and summarizes the other five: *reducing friction.*

---

1   https://sessioncam.com/how-friction-destroys-the-customer-experience/

Why is this principle so important? Because *friction is what kills the customer experience.* High price doesn't necessarily kill the customer experience. Occasional problems with product or service quality don't necessarily kill it, either. But unresolved friction in the processes we set up for customers will!

WHAT DOES IT MEAN?

When I share that opinion with audiences, I'm sometimes met with skepticism. But consider what the word "friction" actually means. Merriam-Webster offers three definitions:

1. The act of rubbing one thing against another.
2. The force that causes a moving body to slow down when it is touching another object.
3. The disagreement or tension between people or groups of people.[2]

Now, if you think about it for a moment, you'll realize that all three of these definitions overlap as metaphors to perfectly describe a customer service experience gone wrong.

A set of customer expectations rubs up against some obstacle or other – out-of-stock inventory, a preventable delay, an error in shipping, slavish adherence to "the rulebook," the service person's attitude, or any other breakdown in the system. Then what happens? The momentum that the customer had toward buying from us or working with us again slows down – all because the customer ran into that obstacle and we didn't do anything meaningful to stop it. As a result, there is unresolved

---

2   https://www.merriam-webster.com/dictionary/friction

disagreement and/or tension in the relationship. These three definitions show us how failure to deliver an above-average experience to the customer typically translates into friction ... and customers hate it.

CONVENIENCE INSIGHT

_____

Friction kills the customer experience - and those who do the best job of reducing or removing it are most likely to win in the marketplace.

THE OPPOSITE OF FRICTION

Taking into account the definitions we've just examined, the opposite of friction would be something like agreement, peace, harmony or ease. And guess what! That's what customers are after: the opposite of friction. After all, wouldn't most of us agree that if we were given the choice, we would prefer to have a customer experience *without* friction – one that is *easy?*

I think that's the best word to focus on – easy – when it comes to understanding how vitally important reducing friction is to business operations in today's environment. The antithesis of an experience with friction is one that is *easy* for the customer.

CUSTOMERS HATE FRICTION IN BUSINESS

All of us are customers; that means all of us can "get" this concept on a personal level. We all hate friction when businesses serve it up to us and don't do anything to minimize or eliminate it. Sometimes we accept friction grudgingly. Sometimes we put up with it. But we never *like* it. Unfortunately, friction happens to us quite often, sometimes multiple times during a single day.

Friction is when we're put on hold for too long.

Friction is when we're on the phone with a customer service agent and we're transferred to someone else, and we have to explain our issue all over again from scratch to a new person, sometimes three or four times in a row.

Friction is being stuck in a long checkout line.

Friction is dealing with traffic in a crowded parking lot.

Friction is when we expect an item to be delivered on a certain day and it doesn't arrive.

Friction is the sales rep who shows up late for a meeting.

Friction is having to put up with a long delay at the doctor's office, even though we showed up on time.

Friction is the cable TV guy who doesn't show up on time, even though we had to take a day off from work to make sure we were there for the appointment.

In short, friction is something that makes doing business with someone anything other than easy.

BE A DISRUPTER

If you like, you can substitute the word "easy" for the word "convenient." But whatever word you use, the main point remains the same: when we come up with an easier, frictionless way to do business with our customers, we are more likely to establish a powerful competitive edge in the marketplace. Reducing friction is more important than lowering the price, and it's more important than redesigning your product or service; it's what creates sudden, enduring marketplace dominance; it's the cornerstone of the 21st century marketplace advantage.

This kind of advantage can help you disrupt an entire industry ... or maybe just help you disrupt your competition down the street. It's all up to you.

So, start by asking some simple questions: Where are the friction points in our business? Where do we find that our current way of doing business creates a situation that habitually "rubs customers the wrong way" – by slowing down their progress, giving them one more hassle that they didn't need, or even giving them a cause for complaint, tension, or disagreement?

Before you say you have no friction points, let me ask you this: have you *asked* your customers whether there is anything about their experience with your business that they would change?

Once you start that conversation, I predict you're going to find that what your customers really want is an experience that is *easy* ... which means no hassle, no problems, no friction. If you think that's an impossibly high standard, read on. In this section of the book, you'll find powerful examples of companies that listened hard, identified friction points, and found a way to get their organizations closer to fulfilling an inspiring vision – a vision of a world where everything is easy for the customer.

CONVENIENCE REVOLUTIONARY PROFILE: UBER

"Uber your business before it gets Kodak-ed."

- ANONYMOUS

The first and, arguably, most important thing to notice about the Convenience Revolution is its capacity to disrupt whole industries. It's hard to think of an example more telling in that regard than Uber, the company that invented ridesharing mobile apps and transformed the modern public transportation landscape.

Before Uber came along, if you wanted to get somewhere in a city and you didn't want to drive or take a bus or train, your most affordable option was to get a cab. You might have waited for one to drive by or called ahead. The point is, typically, there was a lot of waiting involved. Once a cab came along, you hopped in, were driven to your destination, and you paid the driver a rate that was mandated by local regulations and that the (licensed) cab driver had to abide by. You fumbled around for a bit, pulled out your cash or a credit card, and arranged for payment before you left the vehicle. If you felt like it, you tipped the driver.

What happens today? Well, if you use Uber in its most popular incarnation, as a "dynamic pricing" transportation service, you pull up the Uber app on your smartphone or computer, enter your destination, get a quoted fare, agree to it, and the driver shows up shortly thereafter. And, you can use that same app to track when your driver will arrive.

Since you've already set up the payment info on your Uber account, you don't have to fumble around for anything when you get to where you're going. You simply get out and get on with your day. If you feel like it, you tip the driver later, again using the app.

The difference between the two experiences – and the reason behind Uber's astonishing levels of success – can be summed up in two words: *reduced friction.*

At this stage, of course, there are a lot of other things that need to be said about Uber. I can think of three. First, let's note that what you've just read is not the only service it offers; you can arrange multiple kinds of rides, even for large groups. You can also set up ride shares and food delivery. Second, Uber has stepped on a lot of toes. Remember what I said a little earlier about disruption, about how convenience can disrupt entire industries? Well, cab drivers and others invested in a pre-convenience, higher-friction urban transportation model have had their share of complaints about Uber. Third, the company has had several high-profile leadership problems.

All of that is interesting. All of that is worth taking into account. None of that changes the basic reality: Uber figured out a way to *significantly* reduce the friction experienced by taxicab customers. Five billion rides later, it's a fixture of daily life in more than 600 municipalities and 24 countries, and it continues to grow.[3] The company (still privately held) is worth over 6 billion dollars. Not bad for a company in the taxi business that doesn't own any vehicles!

What the leadership at Uber noticed, and acted on, was something countless cab riders already knew all too well from personal experience: it's sometimes way too hard to get a cab.

---

3   https://www.uber.com/en-SG/blog/uber-hits-5-billion-rides-milestone/

Enter Uber's dynamic pricing model, in which the rider is quoted a price that's not based on a set rate, but on the laws of supply and demand that drive the entire capitalist economy. Unless demand is very high, the price of an Uber ride is typically a little less than a cab. When the rider agrees that the price is right, the ride is arranged. Bottom line: reduced friction.

That's not all. The folks at Uber also noticed that users of taxicabs are often in a hurry to get where they're going. So they asked another question: *what can we do to make the rider's life easier and more hassle-free?* Answer: take care of payment ahead of time … and make tipping optional, something that not only depends on how the rider felt about the service delivered, but that also happens after the ride is finished, winning back valuable time and removing a layer of social pressure to tip every driver. Bottom line: reduced friction.

You can say that you like Uber and that you think it's a brilliant idea. You can say that you hate Uber and that you think it's the end of civilization as we know it. I have my own opinions, and I know what I'd say about the customer experience the company has created, having used the Uber app more times than I can count. What hundreds of millions of riders say with the combined voice of their purchasing decisions is what really matters, though. And *nobody* can say riders don't care for Uber. They love avoiding that taxi cab friction. They keep right on choosing Uber, whether that's popular with cab companies or not.

Just like Apple disrupted the music industry with the iPod and its later streaming music options, Uber disrupted the cab industry. And just like Apple, it has its share of competitors within the new environment it created, Lyft being the most prominent. No one is saying the company is perfect, or that any company is perfect. What needs to be noted, though, is that companies like Uber, companies that aggressively raise the bar in the area of reducing friction, are the ones that get the biggest say in what happens next ... and reap the biggest rewards.

POTENT QUOTE

"Uber is convenient; it's easy to use and to pay with a credit card. You can even split the fare with other passengers. Credit card payment is a game-changer for me since I've been frustrated several times because of taxis that don't offer the option or whose machines malfunction. The receipt is emailed to you, and that is a great relief to my receipt-stuffed wallet."

– FREDERIK ROEDER, IN DEFENSE OF UBER

REDUCING FRICTION SNAPSHOT: THE RUHLIN GROUP

The Ruhlin Group describes itself as a "gift strategy and logistics company." That's another way of saying they pick out and handle *all* elements of gifting for a company – not just selection of the gift (a decision which can often have major strategic implications), but also writing the note, shipping the gift and personalizing the entire experience. They are a concierge service that identifies highly targeted, world-class gifts that can cut through the noise, increase referrals and increase retention with the most important clients, employees and prospects, so you don't have to.

A lot of people are surprised that such a company exists. Who needs help picking out gifts? But business gifting strategy is very serious business, as the firm's roster of blockbuster A-list clients (the Chicago Cubs, Wells Fargo and Shell, just to name a few) suggests. As founder John Ruhlin, author of *Giftology*, sees it, the goal is to identify just the right person to receive just the right gift – ideally, a gift that will resonate with both the recipient and his or her family, and thus strengthen the relationship over time. That takes time, effort and insight – and a lot of company leaders simply don't have the bandwidth. As it turns out, the answer to the question "Who needs help picking out gifts?" turns out to be "Anybody with a major client worth keeping or a key employee worth holding on to."

So, if you're the Chicago Cubs, what *do* you give to your top corporate sponsors and the people who buy the elite corporate box seats and luxury suites at Wrigley Field? If you said, "Send everybody a Cubs calendar," go to the back of the class. If you said, "Send everybody a fancy fruit basket," go even further back. It's the thought that counts, and neither of those options show much thought, uniqueness or care. Here's what the Ruhlin Group came up with for each of the Cubs' top-tier business allies: a top-notch Bluetooth speaker set into a casing built using wood salvaged from the Cubs' original locker room, constructed in 1914. That beats a fruit basket any day of the year ...

and you'd better believe an upscale Cubs fan will mention that gift and show it off to friends and family.

The Ruhlin Group streamlines the process of business gifting. Its clients have one less thing to worry about when it comes to maintaining and improving the quality of their most important business relationships. That means less friction ... and more sales.

POTENT QUOTE

"Ruhlin and his team help companies to identify the top recipients to target among their existing clients and prospects based on such metrics as current and lifetime revenue, referral value, and their specific influence role with the corporate structure. They then turnkey everything else – from selecting, personalizing and creating the gift, determining when to send it, delivering it in a unique way, and handling follow-ups to ensure it hit the mark and achieved its overall objective."

– FORBES

REDUCING FRICTION SNAPSHOT: ACE HARDWARE

I'm a huge Ace Hardware fan and wrote about them at length in my book "Amaze Every Customer Every Time." Ace is that local store that has the helpful, experienced employees who can give you the advice you need to finish your weekend project, help you find that obscure part, and even keep you from buying something you don't need. They are the small, locally-owned stores that compete against home improvement store behemoths that are typically 10 times bigger and spend 30 times more on advertising. In this very competitive market, Ace thrives because of its special brand of customer service, which is all about one word: helpful.

The truly great companies create a signature or brand that supports their vision of customer service. Ace Hardware focuses on *helpful*. It is their tag line as well as their brand promise: they want to be the most helpful hardware stores on the planet. They are "the helpful place." Notice that they didn't say "biggest place" or "cheapest place"!

Ace's positioning as "the helpful place" is a great example of a simple, concise brand statement that promises, and delivers, an amazing customer service experience. It's easy for employees to get what the brand's promise is. It's easy for customers to get it, too.

The stores are incredibly easy to do business with, beginning before you even get in the door! Making sense of the parking lot is much less of a hassle at Ace than it is at the big-box stores. The folks at Ace call this "rock star parking," a phrase I love.

Just as important, navigating through the store doesn't mean a quarter-mile walk from one side of the store to the other. There always seems to be more staff available to help the customers than in the typical big-box store, and you never feel like you're inconveniencing them when you ask for help. Store employees engage customers when they enter the store. Ace associates are taught to ask, "What can I help you find today?" When they find out, they don't just point the customer in the right direction, they walk the customer to the item. That's reducing friction.

Here's another big difference between what Ace does and what big-box stores do: checkout time. This ties into the larger issue of being able to spend less time in the store because you get help finding what you need – fast – and get out fast. As one online reviewer put it, "Convenient, friendly and helpful. Someone always available to assist. Have most of what I need most of the time. Checkout is fast and efficient. Never have to wait long. Certainly prefer this to a big-box store."[4] Add it all up, and you've got a chain of smaller stores taking on the big guys – and winning – by making life easier for the customer.

Ace's sustained commitment to being "the helpful place" translates into serious customer loyalty, a major marketplace advantage in this brutally competitive sector of the economy. A Market Force Information survey of more than 7,800 consumers ranked Ace as the hardware option customers are most likely to recommend to friends and family, and as the No. 1 retailer of choice for home improvement projects. The rankings were based on high scores in ease of shopping, customer service, associate knowledge and fast checkouts – all of which connect to the chain's ongoing campaign to reduce friction for its customers.[5]

---

4   https://www.yelp.com/biz/handyman-ace-hardware-stores-dayton-2
5   http://www.retailwire.com/discussion/why-do-so-many-people-love-shopping-at-ace-hardware/

POTENT QUOTE

"Great local hardware store ... and super convenient and so much quicker than having to navigate the big hardware stores like Lowe's and Home Depot. Sometimes a bit more expensive but usually worth it due to its convenience. Helpful staff too."

– ONLINE REVIEW FOR ACE

REDUCING FRICTION SNAPSHOT: QUIKTRIP

As you'll recall, Southland Ice Company launched a revolution by reducing friction for its ice customers, offering them products such as bread and milk and eggs, thereby saving them a trip to a traditional grocery store. Southland Ice became 7-Eleven, and invented modern convenience store retailing, which now makes up nearly 34 percent of all retail outlets in the United States.[6]

One of the fascinating things you notice about companies that use the disruptive power of added convenience to shake up whole industries is that, eventually, they face competition, sometimes daunting competition, within the very industry

---

6   https://medium.com/@Compliantia/convenience-store-industry-interesting-facts-and-trends-7ed868819eed

they've transformed. That's the free market system at work, and 7-Eleven is a case in point.

Although the company remains a major force in retailing, an iconic and instantly recognizable brand, and the dominant player in terms of total convenience store outlets nationwide, 7-Eleven is *not* the convenience store American customers rank highest in comprehensive national surveys. That would be a regional chain: Tulsa, Oklahoma-based, QuikTrip. It's worth noticing *why* QuikTrip heads that list.

Market Force Information's annual survey of America's favorite convenience stores found QuikTrip to be the clear winner[7] in overall consumer preference, based on its presence at or near the top of the list in the following areas: merchandise quality and selection, payment authorization speed, cashier service, and ease of getting in and out of the store. QuikTrip came in first or tied for first in every one of those categories.

What I want you to notice about the areas where QuikTrip established its competitive edge (and invested heavily in doing so) is that *each and every one of them reduces friction for the customer.* Think about it. If you spend less time looking for what you want in the store ... if your payment goes through more quickly ... if the cashiers throughout the chain are trained to minimize your wait time and deliver courteous service to you (which they are) ... and if you get in and out of the store in a way that delivers the "quick trip" the store's brand promises ... guess what? That makes your life easier. You're going to come back.

---

7   http://www.marketforce.com/new-market-force-study-finds-quiktrip-and-costco-are-america%E2%80%99s-favorite-places-fuel

POTENT QUOTE
———

"Seriously, this place has everything. If you don't have a QuikTrip in your state, I feel sorry for you."

– ONLINE REVIEW FOR QUIKTRIP

REDUCING FRICTION SNAPSHOT: CLEAR

"*Frictionless* describes how we help you travel through life. We think it fits."[8] So reads the website for CLEAR, an expedited airport and stadium security program currently operating in 19 U.S. cities.

Those two sentences made me smile. I researched hundreds of companies for this book; CLEAR was the first one that literally spoke my language. And why shouldn't they? This is a company whose entire business model is built around the idea of removing hassle and inconvenience from the customer experience. Its website continues with a simple, direct answer to the question that's probably on your mind right now: What exactly do they mean by "frictionless" travel?

Glad you asked.

CLEAR Membership: Your key to airports, stadiums, arenas and more. Verify who you are with a tap of the finger

---

8   https://www.clearme.com/home

or blink of an eye. You're CLEAR. Speed through security lines in five minutes or less. CLEAR speeds you through the long line for ID check, and guides you to the screening line.[9]

That's what they mean. I have no way of knowing whether you're a frequent flyer, but as someone who is, I'm here to tell you that I'm intrigued by the possibility of winning back some of the time that's lost forever when I'm forced to navigate the cumbersome, hurry-up-and-wait security lines in crowded airports.

Here's how CLEAR works. For an annual membership fee, you sign on with CLEAR and take part in a simple enrollment process at one of their facilities, and it puts you in the fast lane at major U.S. airports and some stadium venues. An easy-to-use kiosk lets you prove who you are with a quick fingerprint or retinal scan. Once you've used this cutting-edge technology to confirm your identity, you're escorted to the front of the security line where you put your carry-on items through the X-ray machine. No waiting in a long line for someone to check your boarding pass and identification documents.

In a sense, CLEAR competes with the Transportation Security Administration's various Trusted Traveler programs, each of which charge a lower registration fee than CLEAR does and provides similar expedited security screening benefits. Lots of travelers use both systems, also.

Now, you might wonder why someone would choose to pay more for what looks like the same service. Here's the short

---

9   http://clearme.com

POTENT QUOTE

"CLEAR members enjoy more predictable access to security, which means those who check in online and don't check bags can schedule airport arrivals even closer to departure than they would normally. Otherwise, you can still spend more time in your favorite lounge or restaurant, and less time waiting in line for the TSA. ..."

– DEAN TAKAHASHI IN VENTUREBEAT

answer: they're not really the same ... because CLEAR removes more friction than TSA does.

Unlike TSA's PreCheck program, CLEAR customers are never randomly excluded from the expedited system and told to check in through the standard line. They're always in the fast lane. A second reason is the simple one that, since the fee is higher, CLEAR lines are predictably shorter. In addition, there's the obvious difference that TSA doesn't get you into Yankee Stadium any faster than other ticketholders, while CLEAR can.[10] The prospect of streamlining your "check-in" to a concert, sporting event or other stadium gathering is probably

---

10   http://fortune.com/2015/08/07/yankees-biometrics-stadium-clear/

almost as cool as the prospect of getting through security in five minutes or less.

CLEAR doesn't fix everything that's become inconvenient about flying, but it does get you past the first step of the security screening process faster, more predictably and less stressfully than you'd otherwise be able to manage.

REDUCING FRICTION SNAPSHOT: GOOGLE

This entry could easily have gone into the Technology portion of the book, but Google has changed the game in so many different areas of daily life that it seemed appropriate to include here, in the broader category of Reducing Friction.

Consider just this one aspect: once upon a time, you needed physical access to a printed encyclopedia, the Reader's Guide to Periodical Literature, and a whole host of other heavy, hardbound books if you were serious about researching a topic. You typically found those books at the library, which meant the library was where you had to go whenever you were serious about finding the answers to important questions. That meant driving or walking or taking a bus or finding some other way (not Uber!) to get to where all the books were kept. That seems like a very long time ago indeed.

The reason it seems like such a long time ago, of course, is that a search engine called Google came along in 1998. Google's top-secret algorithm made finding the right information online about virtually anything significantly easier and more convenient than the other engines of the era, sites like Lycos, Yahoo and Webcrawler. The secret Google algorithm has been

tweaked hundreds of times since then, but what matters most
to Google users remains the same: *type a few words into the box,
hit "Return," and you'll find what you're looking for online, easily
and quickly.*

A lot has changed since 1998; Google has driven much of
that change. The company's unrivalled dominance in the search
engine arena supports a profitable digital advertising business,
currently generating over $73 billion a year, which translates
to roughly one-third of all digital advertising on the planet ...
driven by a single company.[11] That's an extraordinary achievement, one that was (and is) driven by Google's commitment
to make the computer user's online experience easier and
more convenient.

The hammerlock on competitors that Google now holds in
the realm of online search has allowed the company to bring
its distinctive user-friendly, friction-free tech vision to an offering of nominally free products that move users beyond online
searches. These include applications for email (Gmail/Inbox),
work and productivity (Google Docs, Sheets and Slides), scheduling and time management (Google Calendar), cloud storage
(Google Drive), social networking (Google+), language translation (Google Translate), mapping and turn-by-turn navigation (Google Maps/Waze), video sharing (YouTube), and
photo organizing and editing (Google Photos), not to mention
the Android phone and Chrome browser, each of which dominates its market.[12] [13] By the way, if you use the Chrome browser,

11   https://www.recode.net/2017/7/24/16020330/google-digital-mobile-ad-revenue-world-leader-face-
     book-growth
12   https://www.idc.com/promo/smartphone-market-share/os
13   http://gs.statcounter.com/browser-market-share

every one of those applications eventually leads you back to the search engine that an estimated 78 percent of all online users on Earth choose first: Google.[14]

POTENT QUOTE

"Of course, the number one reason for Google's greatness is its super-fast and extraordinarily thorough web search. There is something so reassuringly familiar about using Google's search engine facility. The first page of results is usually all you'll need and the little summary following the main hit is ideal to decide if a site is click-worthy."

- "8 REASONS WHY I LOVE GOOGLE" FROM ALLWOMENSTALK.COM

---

14   https://www.netmarketshare.com/search-engine-market-share.aspx?qprid=4&qpcustomd=0

THE TAKEAWAYS

This principle leads the list because everything this book covers is a variation, in one way or another, on the idea of removing friction from the customer's world. Some companies make reducing friction the central operating principle of their organization.

All things being equal, the customer will gravitate toward the option that is easiest to use. Reducing friction is the tie-breaker. It doesn't have to be the heart of your business model ... but it *should* be something you use to set your organization apart from the competition. In some cases, customers are willing to pay a higher price for reduced friction.

Uber is one of many major brands that owe their success to a willingness to use the reduction of friction as a primary differentiator in the marketplace. Notice that Uber has disrupted and dominated an entire industry by using this strategy.

Before you move on to the next chapter, give yourself some time to write down answers to the following questions. You may not have an answer for each one, but if you take the time to ponder them, you may discover an answer you hadn't previously considered.

- What friction do your customers currently experience? Consider waiting for a cab and fumbling around for money as examples of friction.

- What can you change about your internal or external processes to make your customers' experience easier and more hassle-free that they might be willing to pay a little more for?
- Even though many customers may be willing to pay a little more for convenience, is there a way you could make their experience easier and more hassle-free ... and end up charging *less* than the competition?

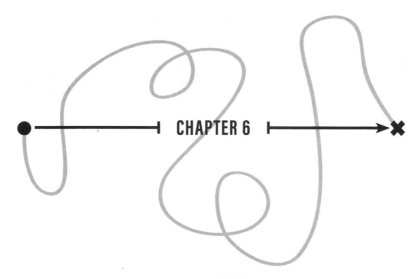

CHAPTER 6

An In-Depth Look at
Principle Two: Self-Service

"Self-service technologies can help firms reduce labor costs while providing more channel options ... but customers must be convinced of their value before foregoing a full-service alternative."[1]

– JOEL E. COLLIER AND SHERYL E. KIMES,

Only if It Is Convenient: Understanding How Convenience Influences Self-Service Technology Evaluation

---

1   http://scholarship.sha.cornell.edu/cgi/viewcontent.cgi?article=1830&context=articles

Putting customers in control gives them power. It allows them to have the kind of experience they want – faster or slower, with interaction or not, for products they've ordered many times or something they've never ordered before. As long as the self-service process in place has been tested properly and does what it's designed to do, the customer experience will at least meet expectations ... because the customer can always be counted on to make choices that support those expectations.

As a general but reliable rule, people prefer well-designed self-service systems that are proven to deliver value over alternatives like waiting in line or being placed on hold. The profusion of self-service kiosks and online portals in any number of settings that previously required a human attendant is a testament to the ongoing impact of this principle. But some important cautionary notes are in order about this powerful, ever-more-popular Convenience Principle.

FIRST, BUILD IN A HUMAN BACKUP

Perhaps most important, no effective self-service process should be completely self-contained. Ideally, there should always be a human backup. If something goes wrong with the system, or there's something your customer doesn't understand, or your customer simply has a question and needs to talk to someone about it, there needs to be some way for an actual human being to take control of the situation.

This can be an employee who helps the customer get started on a touchscreen kiosk, a toll-free number the online customer calls if there's a challenge or question that arises, or any number of other options.

SECOND, MAKE IT EASY FOR EVERYBODY

The self-service options we come up with need to be intelligently designed. This is another way of saying that it needs to take into account the human factor. Humans are a diverse group. What is convenient in a self-service system for one person will not necessarily be convenient to another, and we need to take those differences into account as we design our self-service option. In the end, we may find that a single system is not sufficient to appeal to the wide variety of learning and interaction styles we're engaging with.

Many cutting-edge companies are enhancing the convenience they offer customers by providing *multiple* self-service platforms. For instance, one customer may prefer placing a familiar, repeat order with you by means of a simple text message, while another enjoys customizing each order using a full-featured website. In the customer support world, you can provide a simple Frequently Asked Questions section on your website for customers to find the answers they seek, or share do-it-yourself videos on YouTube for customers to watch. Regardless of the approach you take here, the best way to figure out what different groups of customers consider to be convenient about a self-service system is to test everything extensively with control groups before unveiling what you've come up with to the world at large.

FINALLY, DON'T CROSS THIS OFF THE LIST

Don't make the mistake of imagining you're ever going to be "finished" with this. Self-service is an ongoing commitment, not something you cross off a list. The self-service bar is constantly being raised, and the tools are always getting better. Advanced communications and artificial intelligence technologies are now giving consumers higher and higher expectations about the level of support a good self-service system should provide. One particularly exciting area of innovation has been the introduction of keyword-driven "chatbots." These tools have the potential to bring a conversational, human "feel" to automated online chat sessions ... and then seamlessly transfer customers to a human attendant once the exchange moves beyond the automated system's capacity. Many customers do not even realize that this digital handoff has taken place.

That's just one example of how the tools at our disposal are getting better. I don't know what new resources customers will have gotten used to a couple of years from now, and neither do you ... But I do know we have to be ready, willing, and able to upgrade our self-service offerings to accommodate them.

CONVENIENCE REVOLUTIONARY PROFILE: PANERA BREAD COMPANY

> "Anything that offers convenience to our
> guests would only be good."[2]
> **– PANERA CEO RON SHAICH**

One of the central ideas of this book is the notion that friction kills the customer experience – and those who do the best job of reducing or removing it are most likely to win in the marketplace. Let's face it: customers like things that are easy, and why

---

2 http://uk.businessinsider.com/panera-bread-founder-ron-shaich-on-growth-strategies-2014-11?r=US&IR=T

shouldn't we give them what they like? Of course, this "easiness" – also known as convenience – can take many different forms. One of the most powerful forms is a truly customer-friendly, self-service option.

What do I mean by "customer friendly?" I mean a self-service option that lets customers control the transaction/interaction on their own terms, in a way that improves the overall experience, and that never leaves the customer feeling abandoned. This brings us to Panera Bread, which recently positioned itself on the cutting edge of this powerful friction-removal principle.

Panera is a bakery-café restaurant chain with headquarters in Sunset Hills, Missouri, and 2,000 locations throughout North America. They started out as a local chain of St. Louis restaurants, serving great sandwiches, great coffee, and delicious bakery items, and are now among the leading "fast casual" dining options in their market. I've been a fan for a long time, and I've seen firsthand how committed the company is to prioritizing a convenient customer experience.

For years, a guest would walk into Panera, wait in line to place an order with the cashier, and then wait to pick it up at another counter after the food was prepared. One day, however, I noticed a change in the process. After I ordered my food, rather than standing at the counter, waiting for my name to be called, I was handed a vibrating pager. I could sit at a table and simply wait for the pager to go off before going to the counter to pick up my food. The changes didn't stop there. Down the line, the process became even better. Again, I ordered and was given a pager, but rather than having to pick up the food at the counter, a Panera employee brought the food to the table. They had installed a sensor in every table. When the guest places the pager on top of the table, it alerts the Panera team to which table to bring the food. Cool! But the process gets even better.

One morning, I noticed there were several self-service computers with touchscreens where guests could place their orders. This meant customers did not have to stand in line waiting for a cashier if they didn't feel like it. You could step up to one of the kiosks, input your own order, take your pager, then have a seat at your table, where your food would be delivered a few minutes later.

I had the chance to talk to a manager at the Brentwood, Missouri, store (a suburb of St. Louis) and ask about the changes. What brought them about? The manager's answer was simple: "It's more convenient for the customer." He told me that the inspiration for the kiosks was noticing (key word!) that customers ended up spending a lot of time in line waiting, when they could have been at their table connecting with friends, drinking coffee, reading, or doing just about anything more enjoyable.

The Convenience Revolution continues to transform the customer experience at Panera. It's always been a self-serve type of restaurant, and continues to be. However, computerized kiosks and a better delivery system make the experience easier, faster, and, ultimately, better for the consumer.

The payoff goes beyond a more convenient experience and a happier customer base. Accuracy has improved. As Panera started to roll out the new system almost two years ago, founder and CEO Ron Shaich told *Bloomberg Businessweek*, "The dirty little secret in the food industry is one in seven orders is wrong. We're one in ten, a little better than average. Half of those inaccuracies happen during order input." Shaich also told *USA Today* that employees would not lose their jobs to the new technology. While the computerized kiosks have cut the number of cashiers needed in their restaurants in half, those employees are now delivering food to the customers' tables, thereby creating a better customer service experience.

Notice that there is always a human being available and ready to step in and help if a customer has a problem with placing an order. That's called building in a customer-friendly backup plan, and it's entirely in keeping with Panera's business philosophy. The company was built on principles of convenience and easy access to its employees, even before the ordering innovations. Employees walk around the dining room dealing with customer concerns. Panera's stated aim is to be "An Everyday Oasis," a safe, welcoming place where customers can meet with friends and family, hold meetings or be alone – and always on the customer's terms.

Sometimes when a company implements a new self-service solution, that solution ends up creating a negative experience for the customer. Some grocery chains, for instance, rolled out self-service options without doing the field testing necessary to figure out whether customers liked the systems, found them easy to use, or would use them as they were designed to be used.[3] Bottom line: customers may struggle to get used to a new self-service system, or may come away from the experience feeling that they have been left without a backup option.

Panera didn't make these mistakes! As they rolled out the

---

3   https://www.cnbc.com/id/44668419

kiosk concept at the Brentwood store I visit almost weekly, there was always a team member there to help and teach customers how to use the system. And the reward for every customer who tried the new system – in addition to avoiding long lines – was a free coffee or soft drink. So, in addition to teaching the customer how to "behave" in the future, as in using their kiosks, Panera also rewarded that behavior. Chalk it up as a win for the customer ... and a win for the company.

Today's "fast casual" customer expects a good meal, a fair price and good customer service. When a competitor offers and meets the same expectations, there is one more competitive

---

POTENT QUOTE

"As the (kiosk) system allows for more employees in the kitchen, the wait isn't any longer – if anything, it's slightly shorter. ... You can also order on the Panera phone app and pick up at the restaurant, skipping the kiosks. ... And of course, the food is still delicious – nothing has changed here. Steaming hot! So, while human contact may have decreased at Panera, the eating experience is ultimately the same."

– HOLLIS JOHNSON IN BUSINESS INSIDER

weapon at a company's disposal: convenience. All things being equal, the company that is more convenient will win. Panera leads the way in self-service because it continues to leverage convenience in a way that creates a competitive advantage. Its smartphone app, for instance, allows customers to place orders ahead of time via "Panera Rapid Pickup" and get their food on arrival. Some Panera locations even offer delivery services!

Panera continues be a truly great role model for the deployment of self-service options that are created, tested and rolled out with the customer in mind.

SELF-SERVICE SNAPSHOT: WALKME

WalkMe is a cutting-edge digital adoption platform (DAP). What exactly does that mean? I had a feeling you'd ask that. . Perhaps the best way to explain what WalkMe does is to take a moment to consider how companies have traditionally tried to support people who want to access self-service websites.

Let's say you're a first-time user who's landed on such a site and you aren't quite sure what to do. What are your options? Well, historically, you've gotten help by calling tech support, emailing a question, or filling out a support ticket form and waiting for a response. Those are common, traditional methods. Then there are the typical self-service options: you might read the Frequently Asked Questions page or watch a video tutorial or study and research articles the company provides about the specific topic you need help with. Depending on how they're designed, the self-service options may be quicker and more efficient than those traditional methods. But is there an even better way?

Enter WalkMe. It removes some of the friction by taking a more hands-on approach to supporting you. As the name suggests, the system walks you through every step with pop-up windows that give crystal-clear instructions in a visually memorable way, showing you exactly what you're supposed to do next to get the outcome you want. This is a web-based interactive platform that can make any self-service environment easier to navigate the very first time.

WalkMe provides a self-service solution that makes self-service itself faster and easier; it shifts the burden of learning a new system away from the end user to the DAP; it removes friction; it makes it easy for you to quickly get to a level of comfort and mastery of the system you're using; and it frees you up to do better things with your time. So, unless you happen to be a big fan of stumbling through unfamiliar help screens, filing support tickets, calling the help lines and being put on hold, or spending yet another half-day in another training program, you'll like using WalkMe.

Let's face it, it's easy to feel overwhelmed by all the digital environments we're expected to understand and use. Sometimes it can seem like the computer wants us to adjust to its way of looking at the world. This company's motto is "Systems should adapt to us." That sentiment is a great starting point for the achievement of a noble goal: dramatically reducing the hassle that comes along with mastering a new online learning curve.

POTENT QUOTE

"I can and have created customized walk-throughs for our customers to utilize to learn different tasks within the software. Overall, WalkMe is just fun, which is not something that is easy to do. Connecting customers with resources feels very rewarding for both parties involved."

- USER REVIEW OF WALKME ON SOFTWAREADVICE.COM

SELF-SERVICE SNAPSHOT: IKEA

IKEA, the global €36.4 billion ($42 billion)[4] furniture and housewares giant, is one of the great and enduring retail success stories. Founded in Sweden in 1943, the company has been the world's largest furniture retailer since at least 2008.[5] At last count, more than 900 million customers a year made their way into an IKEA store. Most of these stores are not centrally located in urban centers, which means that you often drive a fair distance to get to one.

Here's the amazing part: if you're an IKEA customer, once you do all that driving, you typically *aren't* showing up just

---

4   Dollar to euro rate as of October 10, 2017
5   https://www.forbes.com/sites/walterloeb/2012/12/05/ikea-is-a-world-wide-wonder/#6e094d527b9b

to examine the merchandise. You're showing up with the specific intention of buying furniture *that day*. And that's exactly what customers have been doing in ever-increasing numbers. According to the latest figures, IKEA's sales were up a robust 7 percent over the previous year.[6] That's a number a lot of other retailers would like to be able to achieve, but can't.

How does IKEA do it? By building convenience, and specifically, self-service, into a customer-focused business model.

IKEA makes self-service the central element of a memorable, destination-driven, family-oriented shopping experience. It lets customers meander through showrooms, jot down product codes, and then pick out their own merchandise in what might elsewhere be called a warehouse. It's the customers that move the goods out toward IKEA's massive checkout lanes. (Yes, that means the customers are performing the labor that other retailers pay warehouse employees to do.) Customers assemble and deliver their own furniture – but they can pay to have it delivered and assembled by professionals if they want.

Most people aren't intimidated by the assembly process. Although the visually-driven instruction sheets for those millions of flat-packed furniture kits have received their fair share of parody, they're actually quite user-friendly. The furniture is relatively easy to put together, it's inexpensive but not cheap, it targets customers who want to make the most of a small budget and a small living space, and it's designed to be replaced every five years or so, which matches the fast-paced lifestyle of the customers that IKEA targets. The experience of buying this

---

6   https://www.ft.com/content/6dc5c7c9-a252-3fc2-9401-7fb45f8e064a

furniture is – who knew? – enjoyable enough to schedule a full weekend day around it, even with kids in tow. Many IKEA stores are major social centers, complete with restaurants and children's play areas.

The customer-friendly setting is a blast, and every store is well designed, but the value proposition that has carried the day for IKEA is not "come have Swedish meatballs at our

---

POTENT QUOTE

"Strive for convenience: IKEA invented flat-packed furniture more than 50 years ago after a product designer was having difficulty storing a table in his car and came up with the idea of taking the legs off. Today, the majority of IKEA's products come in flat packs with instructions, allowing customers to assemble the furniture with simple tools. The space-conserving design makes the products relatively easy to transport, both during the manufacturing process and after being sold."

– GRAHAM WINFREY, The Design Secrets
that Turned IKEA into a Furniture Heavyweight in INC.

restaurant." Instead, it's rooted in the company's distinctive self-service offering. Customers can get high quality furniture with a clean and simple design at an extremely competitive price ... and they can *control* the process of delivery and assembly. By the way, that's a crucial word in any successful self-service option: *control*.

The company also boasts world-class support for customers who need assistance, including a 24/7 web chat option. Put it all together and you've got a high-value, self-service experience people love in both its online and in-person forms ... and come back for again and again.

SELF-SERVICE SNAPSHOT: SALESFORCE

Customer relationship management (CRM) is a $26 billion business,[7] and Salesforce.com, best known for its state-of-the-art interface for sales teams, is the reigning leader of the pack. The first company to bring mobile computing to CRM[8], thereby liberating millions of salespeople from their cubicles and desktop computers, Salesforce has an enduring commitment to the development of robust, intuitive, user-driven platforms. Ease of use, autonomy and portability are at the heart of the company's operating philosophy.

Salesforce even creates self-service portals for other companies. Cool factoid from Salesforce.com: 39 percent of millennials check a company's Frequently Asked Questions page first when they have a question, showing a "clear preference for

---

7   http://www.gartner.com/newsroom/id/3329317
8   https://www.fool.com/investing/2017/08/24/3-insightful-quotes-from-salesforcecom-inc-managem.aspx

finding answers on their own"[9] – that is to say, a clear preference for self-service.

Long story short: these people are very, very good at self-service in the digital realm, and perhaps the best in the business.

It's interesting, then, to look at one of the tools this industry leader has chosen to deploy as part of its comprehensive customer support offering. Salesforce uses YouTube, the most public digital outlet there is, as a service support platform. The company's YouTube channel has more than 86,000 subscribers and offers over 1,000 professionally-produced videos ranging from brief demos to in-depth instruction sessions, from promotion and product launch announcements to live streams of Salesforce.com conference events. You don't have to pay for any

---

POTENT QUOTE

"This technology is creating cultures where people thrive. That's what Salesforce really provides users, in real time. The power to change and improve, constantly."

– ANTHONY ROBBINS

---

9   https://www.salesforce.com/hub/service/self-service-portals/

of it or log on to the Salesforce website to get access to this channel. It's just there.

Here's what I love about this: it takes self-service into another realm. Not only can customers get focused support and find the right answer to a specific question by watching a brief video, but someone who's only *thinking* of using Salesforce.com can come across this immense archive on YouTube and think, "Wow – look at everything they're offering here." So, the self-service video channel functions as an effective marketing tool as well.

SELF-SERVICE SNAPSHOT: DELTA AIRLINES

I have always been a big fan of self-service systems that really work for customers. As I was assembling examples and case studies for this book, I couldn't overlook the fact that today, the ease and quality of commercial air travel has been much improved by self-service. I don't know which airline did the most to develop today's self-service systems, and I suppose.it doesn't really matter. I'm building this chapter around Delta, since Delta is the airline that inspired one of my all-time favorite customer stories about self-service.

Here's what happened ... I was talking with a friend about great customer service and he said, "I just had the greatest experience on Delta Airlines. I made it all the way to the gate and I didn't have to talk to one Delta Airlines employee." He smiled broadly.

Now, taken out of context, you might think that was a great experience because he doesn't like dealing with Delta. I asked, "What do you mean? Have you had problems with the Delta employees?"

He said, "Oh no – on the contrary. I fly them all the time and their people are great. The reason this was a top-notch experience lies in what Delta has done to make the whole process easy. They've created a system that allows me to make my reservation and buy my ticket online. The day before the flight I print out my boarding pass at home. And since I'm carrying on my bag and don't have to check my luggage, all I have to do is go straight to the gate. It's so easy. And I know that if there is a problem, I can call Delta or find an agent at the airport who can help me."

That last sentence is important. He knew that if there was a problem, the good people at Delta would be there to support him. As I've noted already, that's an important part of every self-service solution. There must be a backup plan, and that plan should be a human being who can answer your question or help resolve the problem.

My friend's observation serves as confirmation that Delta's purchase and check-in system really does reduce friction and create convenience for the customer. That's the ultimate test!

The big challenge with self-service systems is that sometimes people need a little time and encouragement before they reach a point where they feel comfortable using them. It was all the way back in 1999 when Northwest Airlines (which merged into Delta in 2008) introduced online check-in to their passengers.[10] It took several years before the public became

---

10 https://en.wikipedia.org/wiki/Airport_check-in#cite_note-10

comfortable with the system. The way airlines went about getting their passengers to start using the self-service option is instructive.

My own go-to airline, American Airlines, offers a great example of how the airlines trained the public to start using the system. AA set up a series of incentives (bribes, if you will) to encourage me to rely more on self-service check-in and service options. These inducements were a combination of frequent-flyer miles and price discounts they offered me over a period of several months, so I could get comfortable relying on their new self-service system. The incentives worked. I tried their system and discovered how easy self-service ticket purchasing and check-in was, and how much time I could save by using them. Now they're just part of my routine.

It's important to note that this self-service solution was a win/win for both the airline and its customers. The airline's win

---

POTENT QUOTE

"Delta's been my go-to airline for a long time now. ... The self-check-in and baggage drop is efficient and convenient. I love being able to select my own assigned seat."

— ONLINE REVIEW FOR DELTA

came in the form of cost savings. Investing in a system to create a self-service solution was expensive up front, but that investment eventually saved the airlines a lot of money. The customers' win was the significant benefit of convenience: no longer having to wait on hold and wait in long lines at the airport.

SELF-SERVICE SNAPSHOT: STARWOOD HOTELS

Just as Delta and other airlines are leveraging technology to make air travel more hassle-free for flyers, in 2015, Starwood Hotels unveiled "the industry's first keyless entry system"[11] for its hotel guests. Starwood thus became the first hotel chain in the world to allow guests to replace their physical room key with a cell phone app that unlocks the door to their room when they want access.

But this is not *just* about keyless entry. It would have been easy to showcase Starwood – and Delta for that matter – in the Technology chapter, but the result of what they have done falls under self-service. Note that the keyless entry system is only part of the self-service system Starwood has designed. Like Delta, Starwood has created a step-by-step process that gives the guest a completely autonomous experience – *if that's what the guest wants.*

Here's how it works: after making a reservation at a participating hotel, you're invited to opt-in to the keyless system 24 hours before you arrive. Once you've opted in, you get a notification that you're already checked in; the app sends you a room number and Bluetooth key when the room is ready, and the

---

11   http://www.sun-sentinel.com/business/tourism/fl-keyless-hotels-20150327-story.html

virtual key shows up on your phone. When you show up at the hotel, you can bypass the front desk, go directly to your room, and hold your smartphone up to the door lock to open it. A green light flashes to let you know the door is unlocked.[12]

There are a number of important things to notice here. First, because Starwood was the very first hotel chain to implement this system, it took the lead in self-service and used the new system to establish a significant marketplace and public relations advantage. (Many other hotels have since followed suit with their own keyless systems.)

Second, look at everything this technology does. The Starwood app harnesses what's known as "state aware" technology,[13] meaning it knows (with your permission) that you're preparing to travel to the hotel or *actually* traveling to the hotel or leaving the hotel. Before your stay, the app can send you information, such as relevant tourist sites or an interactive map link with directions to your hotel. And *after* you show up, Starwood can forward information about setting up dinner reservations and more. Again, *if it's what you want,* you can use the app to set up a total self-service experience from reservation to check out.

Third, and most important of all, *there is always a human backup.* I've already emphasized how important this is. You, the guest, get to automate and speed up all the things that used to steal your time: waiting in line to check in, to get your key, to check out and so on. And if there's ever anything you need from an actual human being, guess what. There's a Starwood

---

employee ready, willing and able to help you in person the minute you reach out. That's the sign of a well-designed self-service system.

It's all up to you. Once you opt in to this system, you still get all the smiles from the staff as you walk through the hotel. You still get all the personality and all the feeling of being welcomed and supported as a valued guest. You just don't have to wait around anymore!

POTENT QUOTE

"Hotels are changing. The status quo is changing. Don't get stuck in the past. Don't be like Blackberry, saying that people will always want to type on a physical keyboard. Do you know what happened to them? I know you do. Let's focus on design and usability. And more importantly, let's focus on what your guests want."

– RONNIE COLEMAN, *Hotel Check-In Technology: It's All about Self-Service*

THE TAKEAWAYS

In many cases, customers prefer doing most things themselves. They are resistant, though, to self-service options that *add* friction to their day, that look like they haven't been thought through, or that appear to be designed only to reduce a company's overhead.

Consider the following scenarios. First situation: You're at a self-service checkout kiosk and the item you want to buy won't scan. There's no one around to help. Second situation: Same self-service kiosk, same issue with the product that won't scan ... but there's a staff member on hand to resolve the issue for you. The first situation fails the convenience test; the second one passes.

Lots of self-service ideas sound good in theory, but end up backfiring. The big question to ask is whether a self-service option makes life easier or more difficult for a customer *in execution.* This means you need to test your ideas before you roll them out on a large scale.

Before you move on to the next chapter, give yourself some time to write down answers to the following questions. You may not have an answer for each one, but if you take the time to ponder them, you may discover an answer you hadn't previously considered.

- At what stage is it *necessary* for your company to interact with your customers? What part of your interaction with your customer could be streamlined by means of a self-service option that lets customers control the transaction/interaction on their own terms?
- Is it possible for customers who prefer self-service to move through the purchasing process without ever dealing directly with an employee?
- What kind of customer-friendly backup plan can you build into your self-service option? If a customer has a problem using your self-service system, how easy is it for them to connect with a human being?

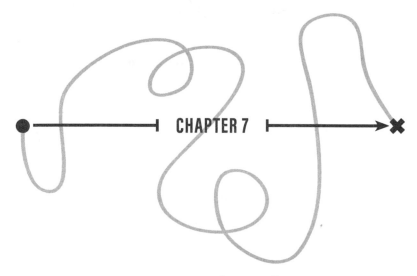

CHAPTER 7

An In-Depth Look at Principle Three: Technology

"Technology made large populations possible; large populations now make technology indispensable."[1]

- JOSEPH KRUTCH

In the broadest sense, technology is any tool you use to accomplish a given objective. In a practical sense, in our time, we've developed a more pragmatic definition of technology: *those tools that I am expected to use regularly that either DO or DO*

---

1   https://www.goodreads.com/quotes/93735-technology-made-large-populations-possible-large-populations-now-make-technology

NOT give me the information, resources and outcomes I need, when I need them.

All too often, the technology we use *doesn't* deliver a positive experience. It adds friction. It makes our lives more stressful and frustrating, not less so.

Marketplace advantage accrues for those who can help customers move from experiencing technology as something that is traditionally inconvenient to something that delivers forward-thinking convenience.

TECHNOLOGY SHOULD REDUCE FRICTION

When our smartphone goes haywire and requires an hour of "tech support" to get back to a useable state, that's friction arising from technology.

When the only ATM within walking distance goes down just when we need to withdraw cash, that's friction arising from technology.

When the company website doesn't bother to pose the question we most need answered on its Frequently Asked Questions list, that's friction arising from technology.

When the online process for resetting a password, making a purchase, connecting with someone, solving a problem, getting cash, sending cash or doing anything else important to us is so complex we feel overwhelmed, that's friction arising from technology.

All of us have horror stories to share about technology gone wrong, and specifically about with regard to communications technology gone wrong with a company that wants our money. We remember those stories, and not for a good reason.

And you know what else? *All* of us love *sharing* those stories about what went wrong with the companies we buy from. We now share those stories with dozens, hundreds, thousands and maybe even millions of other people, via social media. It's one of our favorite topics! So, when there's a technical problem with anything that connects to our user experience, *we are ready, willing and able to share our problem with the whole wide world.* That means potentially major brand damage to those companies that ignore the friction arising from poorly-designed technologies.

Yes, it's true that today's tech gives us the power to do astonishing things. And, it's true that contemporary society wouldn't be recognizable if you took away, even for a single day, all the powerful communications technology that is at our collective fingertips today. But it's also true that most of that communications technology we encounter is not designed to be *easy to use* by customers. Not only that, most of it fails to connect with customers in a focused way that gives them *only* relevant information when they need it. And some of it gives us garbage.

As a result, customers come to assume that the technology they encounter is more likely to *add* friction, often in multiple ways, than to reduce it. And most of the time, sad to say, they're right. Listen to what one fed-up customer had to say about how he felt about dealing with friction that seems to be built into today's technology:

I'm always on some forum or website looking for directions because I forgot how to set it up. Of course, I have to look up my password to do that. Stuff in my car. Stuff in my house. Stuff at work. For the most part, none of these things are overly intellectually taxing on an individual basis, but taken together, I feel like I am at saturation. Too many gadgets, too many passwords, too many directions and instructions and operating procedures to remember. And stuff should just work. There are no moving parts. There is nothing to break. If it worked yesterday, it should work today, but it doesn't, so this thing that was supposed to make my life more convenient is actually sucking time from life.[2]

That's what's happening. That's what your organization is up against. That's the typical reality for today's customer. That's why technology gets a principle all its own in this Convenience Revolution.

THE TECH ADVANTAGE

In this portion of the book, you'll find examples of cutting-edge companies that have leveraged the power of modern technology to make life easier, not more difficult, for the customer; that have found a way to get only the right information in front of the right customers at the right time; and that have used tech to create a positive user experience – the kind that gets people excited about sharing positive things in-person and online.

Technology really can reduce friction in the customer experience, but only when you listen to your customers and use the technology intelligently. Let's look now at some companies that are world-class role models in using technology to create convenience.

---

2   http://gizmodo.com/here-is-everything-that-you-hate-about-technology-1708220141

CONVENIENCE REVOLUTIONARY PROFILE: PAYPAL

"Disruptive technology where you really have a big technology discontinuity ... tends to come from new companies."[3]

– ELON MUSK, founder of X.com, which eventually became PayPal

If you've gotten this far in the book, you know that reducing friction is the name of the game in the Convenience Revolution – because friction is what kills the customer experience.

When it came time to identify a company that successfully leveraged world-class *technology* to reduce friction for customers – and, not coincidentally, disrupt competitors along the way – PayPal immediately leapt to mind. I chose PayPal for one reason and one reason alone: its mission statement explicitly identifies convenience as a critical, strategic goal of the enterprise. PayPal, as you probably know, operates a global online payments system that supports online money transfers and serves as a digital alternative to traditional checks and money orders.

PayPal's company mission is to *"build the web's most convenient, secure, cost-effective payment solution."* Notice that the word "convenient" comes first in the sequence. PayPal has been astonishingly successful in pursuing that mission. You should notice that in pursuing it, the company has developed and deployed its technology in a way that has seriously shaken up the banking and credit card industries, and looks to continue doing so for decades to come. Customers have a lot more choices now than they did back in 1998 when the company

---

3   https://www.inc.com/larry-kim/50-innovation-amp;-success-quotes-from-spacex-founder-elon-musk.html

was founded. They have those choices because PayPal disrupted the market.

That disruption didn't come cheap, and it didn't come overnight. But make no mistake – it happened because PayPal was willing to design, test and roll out a user experience that was significantly more convenient than what was available from competitors. That convenient customer experience is what turned PayPal into a powerhouse.

Of course, it may not be realistic for you to expect your company to deliver technological breakthroughs on the scale of those engineered by companies like PayPal, the kinds of breakthroughs that transform whole marketplaces and turn industries upside down. On the other hand, who knows? Understanding exactly what PayPal accomplished may inspire you to take the steps that allow you to bring about some disruption of your own, on a scale that makes sense for you and your company.

What PayPal accomplished – what turned it into a company with over $10 billion in annual revenue, by last count – can be summarized in two words: *rapid ownership.*

What I mean by that is if you're a customer, it takes you far less time to feel as though you *own* the experience of using and benefiting from PayPal than it takes to feel as though you *own* the experience of, say, using your traditional bank's online portal. In a way, that's an unfair comparison because the bank's online portal does a heck of a lot more than PayPal does. But that's the genius of the technology we're looking at here. PayPal *isn't* a bank. It's taken a tiny corner of what a bank does – make a payment to someone – and made it utterly friction-free.

All you need is the other person's email address. Setting up an account is easy. Making a payment is easy. *Receiving* a payment is easy. There's never a sense of having to wade through 15 different options or having to call tech support. You figure out PayPal in no time. You feel like you own it in a short time. And you are comfortable coming back to it *next* time ... because you quickly own the PayPal experience.

PayPal got big because it made the experience of paying someone, and getting paid, *easy to own*. That's a very big deal when you're talking about technology. Given the constantly-evolving nature of digital communication, making sure this experience stays easy to own is a huge and often expensive undertaking. Why? Because consumer demand, market innovations and security concerns inevitably combine to create an environment in which applications must be constantly updated.

Yet, if you use PayPal regularly (and at the time this book is going to press, more than 200 million people do), you know that it has updated its service while remaining true to its commitment to customers to keep the process easy to understand, easy to master and easy to execute.

It's a sign of the genius behind PayPal's strategic plan, and its willingness to listen to its customers, that the company has managed to add in important new services and capabilities over the years without ever violating that industry-transforming brand promise: *convenient, secure and cost-effective.* For example: in 2015, the company launched PayPal.Me, which allows accountholders to send a custom link requesting payment via text, email and other messaging platforms. More recently, it enabled users to add cash securely to their accounts at their local 7-Eleven store, another brand built on the principle of convenience. Because of PayPal's relentless commitment to fulfilling that brand promise, banks, credit/debit card companies and competing payment platforms all face a daunting task – they must live up to the simplicity and ease of use that PayPal has built into its user experience over the years.

Just like Uber, PayPal has its fair share of critics and probably more than its fair share of aggressive competitors. I'm not placing the company at the head of the list of technology role models because it never makes mistakes or because it's never had challenges. I've placed it here because it perfectly exemplifies the Convenience Principle I want you to remember as you closely evaluate the way your own customers use technology to interact with your business: if you make the experience easier to own and easier to use, you will have more say in what the customer expectations are than your competitors do. As a result, you will be better positioned to meet or exceed those expectations.

POTENT QUOTE
———

"I've never had any problems, the interface is cool, and it just makes my life easier."

– ONLINE REVIEW OF PAYPAL

TECHNOLOGY SNAPSHOT: SQUARE

Square was created in late 2008,[4] when St. Louis glass blower and entrepreneur James McKelvey happened to mention to his friend Jack Dorsey, cofounder of Twitter, that he had just lost a $3,000 sale with a prospect who called in from Panama just because he couldn't accept credit cards from his studio. The two men got to talking about the absurdity of that situation.

McKelvey, a tech guy, as well as a glass craftsman, would later recall that during that conversation he was "struck by the irony of the fact that I was holding in my hand most of the hardware I needed to complete the sale."[5] There they both were, talking to each other on smartphones loaded up with massive computing power, yet McKelvey had been unable to accept a simple credit card order from a remote location. A question emerged: what if there were a portable card reader that small business owners and others could plug into their phones and use to process such orders from *anywhere*?

The friends realized they were onto something and started talking to programmers. McKelvey designed the now-iconic Square card reader, through which cards can be swiped by the phone's owner wherever they are. Dorsey wrote the software for the server that would process the orders. Soon, a new company was born and a needless layer of friction was removed for both consumers and business owners.

The Square card reader, a major technological and commercial breakthrough, accepts credit card payments by connecting

---

4   https://www.technologyreview.com/s/422785/the-new-money/
5   https://www.technologyreview.com/s/422785/the-new-money/

through the mobile device's audio jack. The customer pays nothing, and businesses pay a very reasonable processing fee on each transaction, as any merchant might expect when a customer pays by credit card. Although the card reader is what made the company famous, Square also offers a wide range of other products designed to make life easier for businesses including point of sale software, payroll tools and even some innovative business financing options tailored specifically to companies that use the ubiquitous plug-in attachment. By the way, McKelvey's card reader, a masterpiece of simple, elegant manufacturing design, was inducted into New York City's Museum of Modern Art in 2011.[6]

POTENT QUOTE
___

"With Square, the goal is to get people in immediately, and make the transaction as smooth and simple as possible."

– JACK DORSEY, CEO and Chairman of Square,
CEO of Twitter, and cofounder of both

6   http://newventurist.com/2012/10/who-is-jack-dorsey/

TECHNOLOGY SNAPSHOT: GEICO MOBILE

Auto insurance customers and elite independent ranking services are not what I would call pushovers for good ratings. They don't pass out praise easily. So, it's worth noting that both groups have given consistently high marks to the mobile app developed, supported and relentlessly upgraded by Geico, the Maryland-based insurance company that ranks as the second largest auto insurer in the United States after State Farm. Forrester Research gave the app a nearly perfect score of 96 out of 100, which put the Geico Mobile app at the top of the heap among major U.S. auto insurance apps.[7] Google Play reviews for the app are equally impressive: an average rating of 4.7 out of 5 with well over 100,000 reviews.

The app's high points include a "mobile wallet" that records important information, such as registration, license plates and other vehicle records; the ability to summon GPS-driven emergency roadside assistance right through the app; and a tracking function that quickly lets you know the status of your Geico claim. Since nobody's idea of a good way to spend the day includes looking for paperwork, waiting next to a broken-down car by the side of the road, or waiting for word on what's going on with your claim, it's not surprising that the app has as many fans as it does. The user interface is intuitive and user-friendly.

A side note: customers have come to expect friction-reducing, claim-tracking capacity in their smartphones – and why shouldn't they? We live in a time when Domino's, UPS, Federal

---

7   https://go.forrester.com/blogs/17-05-02-back_to_basics_how_the_most_improved_us_auto_insurers_
mastered_the_mobile_customer_experience/

Express and even the U.S. Postal Service (no one's nominee for the Most Convenient Outfit on Earth award) let customers track items. Doesn't it make just as much sense to let them track their insurance claims? Geico thinks so, and its app serves as a powerful example, not just to the rest of the insurance industry, but for any business currently making customers wait for updates on anything. If you're a retailer, and a customer has placed a special order with you, you could start thinking of ways to make it convenient for your customer to track the status of that special order using a smartphone. Ask yourself: What would Geico do?

POTENT QUOTE
———

"I adore this app! I can do everything I need to do and more. Love the mobile wallet and the fact I can initiate road side service without making a call. Can even change billing info, policy info, and postpone a payment date ... without making a call. I rave about this app all the time – no lie!"

– 5-STAR GOOGLE PLAY REVIEW OF THE GEICO APP

TECHNOLOGY SNAPSHOT: DOMINO'S PIZZA

Ordering pizza delivery has traditionally been one of the most convenient food services available. Yet how many ways has Domino's found to leverage today's communications technology into making pizza delivery even more friction-free for its customers? Let's count them:

1. *Order via Facebook Messenger.* You can chat with Domino's via the Message button on Domino's Facebook page.
2. *Order with zero clicks.* With the special Zero-Click Ordering App, you open the app on your smartphone and let it count down to 0. If you don't interrupt it, your pre-set order gets placed automatically.
3. *Order with Dom.* Via the regular Domino's smartphone app, just sign in, tap on Dom, the voice-activated service icon, and say, "I want my Easy Order." Whether or not you use Dom, you can use the Domino's app to track your order's progress. Pretty cool!
4. *Send a text message.* Just text the pizza emoji, or the words "EASY ORDER," to Domino's SMS short code, DPIZZA (374992).
5. *Tweet.* Tweet #Easyorder or the pizza emoji to @ Dominos. You'll be asked to confirm your order via direct message on Twitter.
6. *Ask Alexa on Amazon Echo.* Amazon Echo is a powerful, hands-free smart speaker you control with voice commands. Alexa is the interface. After you log in to your Amazon account, go to "Skills" and enable the Domino's

skill. Then all you have to do is ask Alexa to place your Easy Order or Recent Order with Domino's.

7. *Order via your Samsung smart TV.* You did know that the coolest TVs (known as smart TVs) come with apps, right? Point your remote at the TV, fire up the Domino's app, and place your Easy Order or Recent Order. You can also track the order on your TV.

8. *Order with Ford Sync.* Driving home? Forgot to order before you left work? No problem. You can connect with Domino's via the voice-activated SYNC AppLink in your new Ford vehicle. Just say "Mobile Apps," then say "Domino's" (that starts up the app) and say, "Place my Easy Order."

9. *Order with your smart watch.* Your Apple Watch, Pebble for iPhone or Android, or Android Wear supports the Domino's app. Just open it and place your order.

10. *Visit Dominos.com.* This seems downright old-fashioned given all the above options, but it still works like a charm, as does visiting your local Domino's in person, if you're so inclined.

Any lingering doubts that Domino's is the single most friction-free, tech-savvy pizza option out there? I didn't think so. (Side note: I could easily have listed Domino's in the Delivery section of this book, given its strong record over a period of decades and the customer loyalty it's inspired in that area. But that wouldn't have been as much fun.)

POTENT QUOTE

"Domino's won me over. ... They made a killer app that complements their awesome delivery service. It's easy to use, intuitive and gives a phenomenal step by step build for your custom pizza. It goes something like this: 1. Select your crust from 5 options 2. Choose your toppings 3. Click through to order additional items and drinks 4. Pay, ka-ching. 5. Get a "tracker" where you watch your order go through delivery stages. Boom. An SMS (text message) announces that the delivery guy is on his way and 10 minutes later a knock on the door."

– DINA CHITAYAT, HAPPY DOMINO'S CUSTOMER

TECHNOLOGY SNAPSHOT: WALGREENS

I've been going to Walgreens since I was a kid. Growing up, I always had a Walgreens just down the street ... and, as luck would have it, there's still a Walgreens down the street from me today! The people working there are still just as nice as they were back then, and maybe even nicer. The company's tagline – "At the corner of happy and healthy" – sums up the way they do business. The pharmacist and I are on a first-name basis, and we always have a few friendly words to exchange.

But it's not just friendliness that has gotten Walgreens to where it is now: a $117 billion chain with more than 8,000 locations. They are sharp retailers operating in a tough, brutally competitive environment. They leverage customer service as a strategy to build customer loyalty. And they've moved confidently into the digital age, exploiting data and technology to create a better, more convenient customer experience.

An astonishing 70 percent of Walgreens' customers now engage with the chain through mobile technology. Half of digital sales come from mobile devices, and more than half the users of the popular Walgreens app are using it while in the store. The payoff is huge. Customers who engage the app in-store *and* online are 3.5 times more valuable than customers who don't. When you add mobile to the mix (in-store + online + mobile), they become six times more valuable![8] [9]

Make no mistake, Walgreens is successfully leveraging technology to transform the customer relationship. This company is creating bar-raising digital experiences across all channels, not just in the store, so customers can make better decisions, save money and have a better overall experience. Of course, different customers interact with Walgreens in different ways. They may interact in the store, from their home computer or over the phone. Walgreens recognizes that it must deliver great experiences across multiple channels, and it does so very well.

---

8   https://www.forbes.com/sites/shephyken/2017/07/08/walgreens-at-the-corner-of-technology-and-a-better-customer-experience-cx/#32b98e4b32c9
9   Interviews with Deepika Pandey, Chief Digital Marketing Officer, Walgreens Boots Alliance

Here's something else Walgreens is doing right: creating special applications that resonate with customers who like to take advantage of technology. A great example of this is the "Refill by Scan" app, which allows the customer to refill a prescription in just 17 seconds by taking a picture of the label on a smartphone. It's fast, easy and convenient, and takes virtually no time to learn how to use.

Bottom line: Walgreens gets it. The company is using technology to make sure it's easy to do business with and to improve the customer experience. In years to come, expect it to continue to raise the technological standard of excellence for its industry.

POTENT QUOTE

"When you are a retailer all about convenience, shaving a few seconds off that checkout experience is huge. All of these little innovations add up to change the customers' experience."

– DEEPIKA PANDEY, Chief Digital Marketing Officer, Walgreens Boots Alliance

TECHNOLOGY SNAPSHOT: NOWAIT

This breakthrough smartphone app allows restaurant patrons to browse nearby restaurants for current wait times, add themselves to a reservation list, receive a text when the table is ready, skip the line, enjoy a meal without the friction of a long wait and even leave a review of the restaurant. In other words, it's a real game changer.

Imagine leaving the house to head out for a nice meal without having any idea where you're going. Your dining companion is skeptical about this plan, but as you head out the door you announce that you've got everything under control. "We'll figure out on the way who has the shortest wait," you say. "We'll pick a great place, and then we'll put our name on the wait list while we're getting gas."

Your dining companion now looks even more skeptical. But as your companion turns the ignition key and heads toward the gas station, you pull out your phone and fire up the NoWait app.

And it all happens exactly the way you said it would.

Diners love the NoWait app because it allows them to put their name on the wait list at a restaurant they like, when they want, without placing a phone call. They can see how many people are ahead of them at any given restaurant and plan their arrival based on the app's estimates, which are refreshingly accurate (I speak from personal experience here).

Restaurant owners who subscribe to NoWait love the app because it helps them better organize their traffic flow, improves the guest experience, and creates powerful analytics that help them manage the business better. And as good as it is for the restaurant, more importantly, it also creates a better, more convenient experience for the restaurant's guests.

To get a sense of the deep personal commitment this company brings to the never-ending task of reducing friction, read the Potent Quote below.

POTENT QUOTE

"When I joined NoWait in 2013 as CEO, the founders suggested I work a couple of hosting shifts seating guests at one of our restaurant chain partners, to witness first-hand the friction our company was working to solve. ... (W)hen the time came to close up, I realized how empowering this experience really was. Right then, it became clear that no one could join our team until they had hosted at one of our restaurant partners — whether they're an intern or an investor."

– WARE SYKES, CEO, NOWAIT

THE TAKEAWAYS

Consider how people *ignore or abandon* technology that isn't easy to use. A classic example of this from years past would be Apple's Newton digital assistant, which claimed to offer user-friendly handwriting recognition, but didn't deliver. It's now an icon of design failure.

Customers' definitions of the phrase "easy to use" will vary, depending not just on their interactions with you, but on their interactions with the best, most intuitive tech that's out there. That means the bar is high, and it's getting higher every day.

PayPal, like each of the companies you've read about in this section of the book, has found a way to use technology to *simplify* the customer's life, rather than make it more complex, frustrating or hard to understand. It looked closely at the ways adults learn, and has found tactics for collapsing the learning curve. Customers spend a comparatively short amount of time getting used to the system, come to feel more confident about using it, and eventually count on it, just like they count on knowing where the light switch is when they walk into a dark but familiar room. That's *ownership*, and the customer's sense of *owning* a given technology is the payoff you're always looking to accelerate.

Before you move on to the next chapter, give yourself some time to write down answers to the following questions. You may not have an answer for each one, but if you take the time to ponder them, you may discover an answer you hadn't previously considered.

- How easy is it for new customers to *own* the technology and information platforms you share with them, and how long does this process take?
- Is there a technological tool that you've seen other organizations using (even if they aren't your competitors) that may be useful to your company? If you could invent any piece of technology to improve the customer experience, what would it be? Is there a comparable option that fits within your budget?
- What do your customers have to say about how easy (or difficult) your technology resources are as a communication platform or as service?

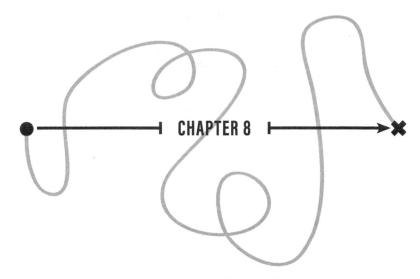

CHAPTER 8

An In-Depth Look at
Principle Four: Subscription

"Four factors – the access generation, light-switch reliability,
delicious data, and the long tail – have led some of the
world's most successful companies and promising start-ups
to shift their business models to a focus on subscriptions."[1]

–JOHN WARRILLOW, *The Automatic Customer:*
Creating a Subscription Business in Any Industry

---

1   https://www.goodreads.com/book/show/22571531-the-automatic-customer

As Warrillow notes in his breakthrough book, which I highly recommend, the subscription model has emerged as a powerful, enduring business model, one whose opportunities are uniquely matched to the times in which we live and work. Here's a quick look at the four factors he identified, each of which could, on its own, serve as a powerful introduction to this dynamic method of reducing friction in the customer experience.

- **The Access Generation** – This phrase refers to an important, and widening, generational gap defined not so much by personal values but by consumer preferences. Specifically, this is about changing notions about the importance, or even relevance, of ownership. In this analysis, younger people value *access* over *assets*, by and large. Thus, the younger you are, the more likely you are to be comfortable with a subscription music service like Spotify than with music you own outright via iTunes or (gasp!) an old-fashioned CD collection. The implications for access to digitally-delivered content, to name only one of a number of potential business areas, are immense.

- **Light-Switch Reliability** – We live in a world where communications, logistics and product deliveries are more reliable than ever before. They're as predictable as flipping a switch and seeing the overhead light turn on. This is not to say that there are never exceptions to the goal of getting consumers what they want, when they want it; I'm saying that when there is such an exception, it stands out to the customer as something that is well outside of the norm. Consistent, on-time delivery of the products and services we want and need is "the new normal." Translation: expectations for ongoing, uninterrupted value delivery are high, and subscription offerings have the potential to meet and/or exceed those expectations, creating a powerful competitive advantage in the marketplace.

- **Delicious Data** – It's no accident that the revenues of companies like Amazon have seemingly grown at exponential speeds over the past decade. That growth is based on the strategically sound use of data as a marketplace weapon. Every time you order something from Amazon (or, for that matter, research something you *might* order from Amazon), Amazon learns something important about who you are, what you want, and what you might want in the future. This information is incredibly valuable and, if collected and analyzed properly, can be used for targeted messaging about subscription offerings that are relevant to your world.

- **The Long Tail** – Our economy has moved away from its traditional focus on a relatively small number of mainstream products and markets at the "head" of the demand curve, and toward a huge and growing number of niche markets at its "tail." If you like something specific – say, a particular variety of gourmet coffee – there's probably someone out there who is willing to build a subscription offering around your eclectic desire.

These four factors combine to make the recurring subscription model a powerful and potentially transformative business offering in virtually any contemporary market. As a result, the question "How can I keep my customers happy by offering a subscription option?" is one that every business, including yours, should, at the very least, consider.

For most businesses, repeat purchases are the Holy Grail of all marketing and sales efforts, for the simple reason that these purchases inevitably cost much less to generate than first-time purchases. The subscription model gives you a way to make repeat purchases *automatic*. Any time a company can automate ongoing revenue, that's a good thing from a business perspective, and a huge advantage for any business model.

You don't have to go that far back to a time when consumers thought about subscriptions as being primarily relevant to magazines and newspapers. Now, consumers buy everything from fresh produce to digital music, from fine wine to clothing, from movies to dog food, by subscription. Businesses now buy office supplies, software, complex digital security solutions and more through subscriptions. There seems to be no limit to the possibilities for the establishment of a competitive advantage in this friction-reduction zone.

There are still many businesses that haven't yet explored this possibility. If you're one of them, you'll probably want to read this part of the book carefully.

BE THE FIRST

Ideally, you want to be the first one to present and deliver on this option for your customer. Here's why: once you've created a recurring revenue relationship by consistently delivering value in a subscription context, you've created a "stickier" relationship with the customer. That means it's difficult for customers to justify moving on to a competitor because of the effort it would take to cancel one account and set up another ... and because of the simple momentum that comes from force of habit.

Customers who subscribe and consistently receive value from their subscription get used to the convenience. They see the process of *changing* vendors as creating friction and, as a result, they tend to stick around.

YOU CAN'T BE GREAT FOR JUST THE FIRST YEAR

People can still get mad and leave subscription arrangements, of course. Anyone with a cable or Internet subscription knows what it's like to sign up for a reasonably-priced service the first year, and then get hit with a big price increase on day one of the following year. This can be a galvanizing experience, the kind that motivates people to start looking closely at the competition all over again.

This is the "gotcha" variation on the subscription model. It's an arrogant approach that assumes the time and effort already invested in the relationship, combined with sheer force of habit, will somehow overcome the unpleasant emotional jolt of having to pay a whole lot more for the same thing.

It's our job to see that customers don't get that kind of jolt in the first place. It's our job to make sure we're using the subscription model to deliver on *all* the value that's been promised, and hopefully, not just meeting, but exceeding expectations. It's our job to follow through on the ease, reliability and consistency that is implied by any subscription relationship. If we do that, customers are going to be happy with us and stay with us, asking only that we remain *somewhat* competitive with our pricing.

On the other hand, if we don't, if we abuse the trust that's been built, the relationship will become adversarial and our competitive advantage will evaporate. Customers will spend a lot of time, effort, and energy arguing about price, or they will simply leave. That's not a great platform for expanding the relationship and developing ongoing revenue. You can't be great for just the first year; you must plan to be great for the lifetime of the relationship.

Intelligently designed subscription offerings can dramatically increase convenience and eliminate friction in the customer's world. They can keep your enterprise competitive and customer-focused. And, they can substantially reduce your cost of sales. In the pages that follow, you'll read about some innovative, best-in-class companies that have deployed smart subscription offerings in a variety of industries to secure a major advantage in the marketplace.

CONVENIENCE REVOLUTIONARY PROFILE: NETFLIX

"Not only does Netflix offer a multitude of movies through their Watch Instantly service, but they also deliver DVDs and Blu-rays right to your door. This is a great convenience because, if you are a film fanatic, you will enjoy 'making of' clips, extra features, director's commentaries and interviews."[2]

– GABRIEL MOURA in *Elements of Cinema, Is Netflix Worth It?*

2　http://www.elementsofcinema.com/general/netflix.html

It's not just movie buffs who are addicted to Netflix's convenience – it's pretty much everybody. This service has transformed the way people consume entertainment. If you doubt that, consider what Cody Wheeler, a blogger and big-league Netflix fan, had to say about the top online streaming service in the country:

> *I actually ditched my Satellite TV service in favor of Netflix recently. I use rabbit ears to pick up local TV channels and ESPN3 to get sporting events. … Being a huge advocate of productivity and time management, I really hate when something or someone wastes my time, which is exactly what most commercials do. With Netflix, I don't even have to fast forward … Netflix technology learns what I like, and adapts to my tastes. Through the user rating system and tracking a history of what you watch, Netflix suggests movies and shows that it thinks I'll like. It gives me categories that are similar to my tastes, and even presents me with a Top 10 of what it thinks I'll really like, which is usually spot on. … That's some amazingly data-driven technology there, and something that only the big dogs of the tech world can ever hope to match.[3]*

It's not uncommon for customers to go into this kind of passionate detail about why they love Netflix, the massively popular subscription video streaming service that lets you instantly watch movies and TV shows online. Notice how *convenience* drives the modern love affair with the Netflix experience. That's

---

3   https://academysuccess.com/top-9-reasons-why-i-freaking-love-netflix-and-why-you-should-too/

what animates Wheeler and millions of other Netflix users, and that's what has turned Netflix into an entertainment powerhouse, boasting a staggering 75 percent share[4] of U.S. homes.

Convenience has always been the company's competitive edge, and understanding how Netflix has evolved over the years offers an important lesson in the deployment of convenience as strategic marketplace leverage.

It's hard to remember now, but Netflix started out small, and it had nothing to do with video streaming. The company was launched back in the late 1990s by Silicon Valley entrepreneurs Reed Hastings and Marc Randolph. Hastings and Randolph watched a lot of videos and, as customers, noticed a chink in the armor of the then-dominant video-rental company, Blockbuster Video. That chink was something you should recognize easily by now: friction.

To put it bluntly, Blockbuster's customers had to put up with a lot of hassle. Hastings has often been quoted as saying that he and Randolph came up with the idea for a DVD-by-mail service after he'd driven all the way to his local Blockbuster, only to be charged $40 in late fees on a VHS copy of *Apollo 13* that he'd kept for too long. So, they decided to take on Blockbuster, the market leader.

Today's researchers believe that it's entirely possible that Hastings created his much-repeated "late fees" story as an illustration of what *might* have happened *had* he held on to a Blockbuster tape for way too long. Hastings was and is a savvy marketer, and the bitter Netflix/Blockbuster market share

---

4   https://techcrunch.com/2017/04/10/netflix-reaches-75-of-u-s-streaming-service-viewers-but-youtube-is-
       catching-up/

battle is now history (Blockbuster lost). So, if he did make that story up, he deserves applause, not criticism. What Hastings captured in that resonant anecdote was a memorable, easy-to-repeat account of the *friction* that Blockbuster built into its business model ... and apparently was doing absolutely nothing to remove, despite mounting customer dissatisfaction.[5]

In 1998, the year Netflix was founded, Blockbuster's huge customer base was experiencing the hassle of having to drive to a physical location during prescribed hours to physically return a video, and paying (often-excessive) late fees when videos weren't returned on time. Blockbuster's management didn't show any signs of noticing (or caring about) the problem, which made Blockbuster vulnerable.

The rise of easy-to-mail DVDs gave Hastings and Randolph the perfect response to customers who *had* gone through the late fee experience. They used that technological advance to challenge the dominant retail video rental company with an innovative, indeed revolutionary, subscription video service.

With Netflix, you didn't have to drive to the video store or pay late charges. You paid a low monthly subscription fee, selected a list of DVDs you wanted to watch, and the first DVD on your list showed up in your mailbox a couple of days later. You returned it when you were done via postage-paid packaging, and then the next DVD on your list showed up. Easy.

Consumers loved it and Blockbuster came to realize that it had serious competition. By 2005, a relatively rapid timeframe by startup standards, Netflix had turned a profit. It was shipping

---

5   http://www.nytimes.com/2001/06/06/business/blockbuster-settles-suits-on-late-fees.html

out a million DVDs every day ... while Blockbuster began a long, ugly descent fueled largely by customer discontent.

Interesting side note: early in its history at the turn of the century, Netflix management offered Blockbuster the chance to buy its company and its innovative no-late-fees business model for just $50 million. It would have been the bargain of the century, but Blockbuster passed, believing that its large network of physical stores would make it easy to overcome a seemingly insignificant competitor in a "niche market" with an interesting idea and a tiny sliver of the market. They were complacent, they were wrong, they lost precious time ... and they failed.

Ten years later, having unsuccessfully attempted to emulate Netflix's astonishing success with a "no-late-fees" approach of its own, Blockbuster was drowning in debt. It filed for bankruptcy in 2010. This part of the story demonstrates the dangers of letting a competitor attend to the friction you create for your customers before you do. This is a critical lesson on the importance of "rapid response" to customer feedback.

These days, of course, we are likely to think of Netflix as the world's dominant video streaming service, not as a DVD rental company. It certainly is the leader in video-on-demand. What's fascinating to note, however, is that Netflix still serves about 4 million individuals in the U.S. who prefer the larger selection and the extra features available by renting a physical DVD.

The lesson here is equally important: one of the beautiful things about a subscription model is flexibility. Greater flexibility means greater opportunity to remove friction. In Netflix's case, it's been able to revise its convenient subscription offering to attract and retain a massive base of loyal followers for its innovative video-on-demand service, launched in 2007. At the same time, it has retained millions of customers who prefer to pay for physical DVDs to arrive in the mail ... it didn't leave those customers behind. And, *both* groups of subscribers benefit from Netflix's state-of-the-art system for predicting what viewers are likely to enjoy watching, which has always been a critical piece of the value that its flexible subscription model delivers. Netflix's early decision to invest heavily in this system is one of the keys to the convenience it delivers to customers.

One final point: the user-friendly technology Netflix has perfected since 2007 is highly cost-effective from the company's point of view. For the roughly 86 million customers now using its streaming video service, Netflix doesn't have to spend money shipping and processing physical DVDs, or maintain warehouses to house those DVDs. However, *cost-effectiveness alone is not a good reason to commit to a business strategy.* Notice that the technology that drives a customer's subscription experience for Netflix is *both* cost-effective (from the company's point of view) *and* low-friction (from the customer's point of view), as evidenced by the love for the service expressed by Cody Wheeler and countless others.

The moral here is a simple one – if you're looking for ways to cut costs, that's fine, but make sure that at the very least the costs you cut don't add friction or otherwise negatively impact the end user experience. As Netflix has demonstrated, it really is possible to *increase* the efficiency of your spending and at the same time *reduce* friction in your subscription service!

POTENT QUOTE

"When Cowen and Company asked Netflix subscribers why they subscribed to the service, 82 percent cited the convenience of on-demand streaming programming."

– EMARKETER.COM

SUBSCRIPTION SNAPSHOT: THE NEW YORK TIMES

I couldn't exclude the industry that invented the subscription model: publishing. You may or may not be one of *The New York Times's* 2 million-plus daily readers, or care that it's been widely regarded as the "paper of record" in the United States since at least the first decade of the 20th century, or know that it has won more Pulitzer Prizes than any other newspaper in the country. None of that matters for our purposes. What matters is that in 2011 the *Times* blazed the single most important digital trail for newspapers looking to survive and thrive in the digital era. And it did that by reducing friction.

Not long ago, the *Times* was in deep financial trouble, like many other publications, as advertising revenues from both its print and online versions plummeted and it struggled to find a way to get its traditional readership to pay for the content they accessed online. The dominant digital model – one the *Times* could not manage to make work – was the so-called "hard paywall."

Under this system, the only way the reader could access the newspaper's content was to pay for a subscription that gave you access to everything the paper offered and then log in and read. This model assumed that customers would think of the online version of newspapers the same way they had thought of print versions for well over a century: as something that was worth subscribing to or buying in its complete, comprehensive, front-to-back, soup-to-nuts, news-to-sports, editorial-to-opinion format.

The only trouble was that online readers *don't* think of newspapers that way anymore.

They typically wanted individual stories and they wanted them *now*. And with so many competing sources of information available in the digital era, there was another challenge to deal with: readers simply don't spend as much time perusing *any* newspaper as they had just a decade or so earlier. They had Twitter. They had Google. They now have dozens of outlets to go to for news and information.

Readers stayed away from the "hard paywall" in droves. They complained. Some of them even fought back hard against the model online, posting hundreds of links to *Times* articles available from alternate sources – not all of them legal.

In 2011, the *Times* proved it was listening to its customers, and, just as important, proved it was capable of evolving. It pioneered a low-friction option that no one else in the industry had considered: the "soft" or "leaky" paywall. That model has changed the game.

Online readers now get access to 10 *Times* articles per week before their IP address hits the paywall prompt asking them to subscribe; they can also track down an additional five articles via search engine queries before they get turned away. Not everybody knows about that second part, and the *Times* doesn't advertise it, just as they don't advertise the fact that tech-savvy readers can find ways to get around some of the restrictions (those would be the "leaks" in the paywall). This is the way the system operates, though. And guess what? It works. Readers searching for individual stories are now transitioning into subscribers in record numbers. The new approach has been a major success for the paper, and it has led to huge increases in both online subscriptions and circulation revenue.

POTENT QUOTE

_____

"Times2020, a planning document released by the publisher in January, identified the Times as a 'subscription-first business.' Over the past year, digital subscriber numbers have shot up around the industry. ... The Times (recently) added 755,000 new subscribers ... a 65 percent increase, according to its most recent quarterly report."

— COLUMBIA JOURNALISM REVIEW

The easy-to-use, low-friction "soft paywall" the *Times* pioneered has emerged as the dominant model in an industry still struggling to find its footing in a digital world. As a result, the most successful newspaper operations are now relying increasingly on subscription revenues rooted in delivering a low-friction, high-value option for today's picky-but-still-information-hungry readers.

SUBSCRIPTION SNAPSHOT: SPOTIFY

Remember when you had to purchase an album you could hold in your hand in order to play a song you liked? Remember compact discs? I won't even bother to ask whether you remember eight-track tapes, since that would be roughly equivalent to asking whether you remember the wax cylinders Thomas Edison used in the original mechanical recording systems. But you get the point.

Things have changed in the world of music. Consumers now have easy, convenient online access to virtually any song they want, any time they want it, thanks to subscription-based streaming services like Spotify. Unless you're a collector of antiques and curiosities, it's no longer necessary to own a physical disc or a record. What you really want, I am betting, is not a plastic case with a disc inside that you can scratch or lose, but access to the songs you love.

Spotify has taken something people enjoy repeatedly in countless settings – music – and made it virtually hassle-free compared to all previous delivery models. Before streaming subscriptions came along, people had to buy a full album when many times all they really wanted was just one or two songs. That was friction and customers had to accept it.

Now you can just pay a small price per month and listen to any song you want from as many different artists as you want, as many times as they want, whenever and wherever you want.

POTENT QUOTE

"I remember what it was like before portable audio was possible. Yes, I'm that old. I remember when it was close to impossible to discover new music, when the only new music I listened to was played on the radio. And, if I liked the song, I had to listen carefully for the name of the artist. If I heard the name, I had to walk to the music store in town while crossing my fingers, because if they didn't have the album in the store, that was it. It was hard to get new music. Today, music is all about Spotify for me. I use it for hours every single day. I started using it as a free member when I got invited during their beta-period. ... Now, I have been a premium member for about a year."

– JENS P. BERGET, SPOTIFY FAN

That's a lot better for the consumer, who doesn't want to have to buy 17 albums just to get the 17 songs they want. And Spotify's analytics are excellent at predicting and suggesting the *kinds* of songs and playlists that listeners are likely to enjoy, making the discovery of new music that suits your personal tastes easier – and more convenient – than ever.

There's also a bigger picture to consider with services like Spotify. A subscription model that gives access to virtually any music release allows independent musicians to get more attention than they otherwise would. It also makes sure that all the artists who create the music get paid, which was something that earlier "file sharing" sites didn't make a priority. All in all, a win for everyone.

SUBSCRIPTION SNAPSHOT: DOLLAR SHAVE CLUB

In 2012, Michael Dubin founded Dollar Shave Club for one simple, powerful, and compelling reason: he was fed up!

Dubin had enough with the high prices and infuriating customer experience of buying and using razors. Wary of potential shoplifters, retailers often locked razors inside special display cabinets, which meant consumers often had to ask an employee for special permission to even touch the product, which was typically sealed in an unwieldy plastic clamshell package that was difficult to open once you got it home. Then there was the "latest and greatest" syndrome, which required major razor manufacturers to come up with ever-newer, ever-more-intricate "shave technology" (three blades, four blades, five blades, special lubricating strips, special decoder rings – well, you get the picture) as marketing gimmicks. And worst of all, the darn things cost too much!

Add it all up and you get *friction*. By the way, I know not everyone may have felt this way about buying razors. But I'm guessing a solid working majority did. I know I did. Dubin did, too, and he decided to do something about it.

He launched Dollar Shave Club with the vision of making buying razors easier, simpler and less expensive for both men and women. Dubin knew women faced similar challenges as men did, and they paid even more for pink plastic and "feminine" styling that added nothing to the user experience.

Dubin figured that people were always going to need razors, but they didn't appreciate the shifting product offerings, the needless hassle in the store and the high prices. So, why not set up a system in which the razors you want simply arrive in the mail and don't cost an arm and a leg?

In other words, why not make a repeat purchase pattern simpler for the customer by offering a subscription service?

That's exactly how Dollar Shave Club works. You choose the type of blade you want. The first time you receive blades, you also get the handle. After that, fresh new blades are sent to you on a monthly or bi-monthly basis. The company offers three membership plans, which can be upgraded or downgraded at any time. The prices are reasonable, the service is reliable, and the cool smartphone app that supports the whole process just won the Webby award for Best Shopping App.

Dollar Shave Club is built on the concept of reducing friction, and the response from customers has been strong. Today there are more than 3 million subscribers – 20 percent of them women – who all came on board because of *one* entrepreneur who started thinking creatively about how to remove friction from the customer's world.

By the way, that entrepreneur's idea was so powerful that it eventually led to the company being purchased by Unilever for *1 billion dollars!*[6]

POTENT QUOTE

"Received DSC as a gift last Christmas. So glad! I've continued with their service and the App makes shopping, ordering and tracking fantastically easy. They are very responsive to inquiries and I appreciate their humor in advertising."

– ONLINE REVIEW FOR DOLLAR SHAVE CLUB

SUBSCRIPTION SNAPSHOT: BLUE APRON

For decades, grocery stores have offered a convenient solution for their customers who are tight on time and don't feel like cooking: the prepared meal. Some are fancy, some aren't.

---

6   http://fortune.com/2016/07/19/unilever-buys-dollar-shave-club-for-1-billion/

But suppose microwaving a frozen, premade meal isn't what you have in mind. And suppose you have a tight schedule, one that doesn't leave a lot of room for navigating the aisles of the supermarket for all the ingredients. And, suppose you're so busy that you don't remember what you do and don't have in the kitchen cupboard. And finally, suppose you *still* want to serve up something magnificent to the people who really matter in your life. Then what?

Enter Blue Apron. The company's motto is "Food is better when you start from scratch." That vision is about as far away from a frozen TV dinner as you can get. This is an ingredient-and-recipe meal kit service operating exclusively in the United States. Subscribers get weekly boxes that contain all the fresh ingredients for the provided recipes to put together truly great meals. A subsidiary service, Blue Apron Wine, offers the perfect beverage complement!

With Blue Apron, you get absolutely everything you need – except for the salt, pepper and olive oil (they assume you have the essentials). Keep those three simple staples on hand, and you never have to worry about whether you have the garlic powder, the cumin, the chopped tomatoes or anything else. It's all there, it's all fresh, and it arrives on your doorstep once a week. The ingredients are carefully packaged in a refrigerated box, so food stays fresh even if you're not home when the delivery arrives.

Founded in 2012, Blue Apron has now shipped more than 8 million meal servings. It has plenty of competition from other meal kit outfits. Grocery stores such as Whole Foods (now owned by Amazon) are getting into this business. But as far as anyone can tell, Blue Apron has the largest fan base[7] in this rapidly growing sector. Want to know why? Read the Potent Quote below.

POTENT QUOTE

"Oh ... the convenience. Not having to go to the grocery store, making lists, planning out recipes and running right back because you forgot an ingredient. Blue Apron just makes life easy. I always receive my Blue Apron on Fridays, and it's great for weekend eats. It comes to your door in a refrigerated box, and all of your ingredients stay fresh for hours. One time, My Blue Apron box was sitting on my porch for 24 hours, and it was still cold when I got home."

— TARALYNN MCNITT, BLUE APRON FAN

---

7   http://time.com/money/4855511/who-buys-meal-kit-services/

SUBSCRIPTION SNAPSHOT: MICROSOFT OFFICE

Over a billion people use some incarnation or other of the Microsoft Office suite of applications, servers and services; although the software giant offers a variety of different configurations for different markets and different platforms, the familiar core components of Word, Excel, PowerPoint and Outlook have been constants in the suite for a long time. What's intriguingly different in recent years is the *way* businesses and individuals have been buying this product from Microsoft.

For the longest time, you bought Office by purchasing a box – a very expensive box – and you bought a brand-new box whenever it was time for an upgrade. If you were a business, you paid a fee for each "seat" (read: user) who had access to what you bought in that box. But in 2013, the company began offering a more convenient way of using the Office suite: a monthly or yearly subscription model. The new model targeted both businesses and consumers, focused on online downloads rather than purchases of physical discs, and made updates automatic over the life of the subscription.

Microsoft wasn't the pioneer of online software subscriptions by any means, but it did have the advantage of being the industry leader in business and personal productivity software. It leveraged that position to identify and act on an area in which technology and customer expectations had shifted. And, it made the experience of keeping your software up-to-date a lot easier.

In an increasingly wireless world, people like the idea of not having to buy an expensive box for an upgrade to each new version, and they're fine with paying modest monthly and annual subscription fees ... indefinitely. Businesses and individuals have come to count on the core functionality of the Office suite without interruption, and millions of users now take those seamless automatic updates for granted. For its part, Microsoft gets a long-term customer commitment from a rapidly-growing market.

According to the latest figures, there are now 60 million active Office 365 subscribers,[8] and approximately 50,000 small businesses sign up each month. The company's Office Mobile apps, which synchronize with a user's subscription offering, have seen even more explosive growth, with more than 340

POTENT QUOTE

"I use the home edition of Office 365. It costs me US $7.99 per month for five users. Read that again. Five users! So, basically, for the price of one modest lunch at a decent Nairobi restaurant you get five members of your family or friends to use what is arguably the best productivity platform in the world."

— MOSES KEMIBARO, MICROSOFT OFFICE FAN

---

8   https://www.windowscentral.com/there-are-now-12-billion-office-users-60-million-office-365-commercial-customers

million downloads. Users love the convenience of being able to work on the go using a smartphone or tablet. And in a disc-free model, I suspect Microsoft has far fewer problems with noncompliance and bootlegging.

Bottom line: Microsoft has adapted to a world in which subscription is the dominant model – and at the same time, it has substantially reduced the friction its users experience.

THE TAKEAWAYS

Many companies assume that a subscription model is not relevant to their business. Maybe this idea *isn't* relevant to your business. Before you make that conclusion, though, consider closely whether your *competitors* could find a way to make a subscription offering reduce friction for your target customer. If, in the mid-90s, you'd have asked the leadership at Blockbuster Video whether subscriptions were relevant to their business, they probably would have said, "No!" Netflix proved otherwise.

Is it possible that there is some inconvenience your customers (or prospective customers) are experiencing that could be minimized or eliminated by a subscription option? The questions below will help you find out.

Before you move on to the next chapter, give yourself some time to write down answers to the following questions. You may not have an answer for each one, but if you take the time to ponder them, you may discover an answer you hadn't previously considered.

- Consider how Netflix took on Blockbuster, focusing on what it believed was inconvenient in Blockbuster's customer experience, such as late fees that customers may consider unreasonable. Does your organization have any similar weaknesses that could be used by your competition to steal business away from you? If so, what are they?

- What is the single most common complaint you hear from customers? Could this be minimized, or removed altogether, by means of a well-designed subscription model? If you already have a subscription model in place, who is your competition in this area, and what are they doing that might be more convenient for their customers?

- Are there any goods or services that your customers purchase on a regular basis? Can you offer your customers a discount on any goods or services if it means you get reliable, ongoing business from them?

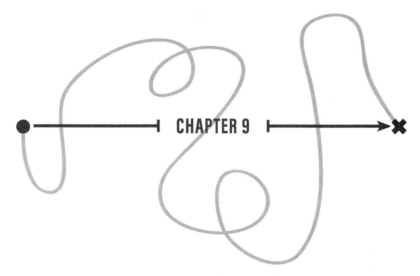

CHAPTER 9

An In-Depth Look at
Principle Five: Delivery

"According to a report by Nielsen, consumers regard online retail outlets as cheaper; they like to compare prices between websites rather than trooping from store to store, and they'd rather have their goods delivered than carry them home."[1]

– SMALL BUSINESS HEROES, *The Rise of Home Delivery*

"**W**hy should I bother thinking about delivering my product or service if delivery service isn't built into my current business model?"

---

1   http://www.smallbusinessheroes.co.uk/features/the-rise-of-home-delivery/#ixzz4ttWCXhpT

"Is delivery really all that relevant to my target customer base?"

"If I've never even considered offering delivery before, should I really have to consider offering delivery now?"

These are all fair questions, and I hear them a lot. There are many business leaders whose initial response when they first encounter this Convenience Principle is, "Guess what. Delivery really isn't relevant to our business."

Here's my response: you may be right. It's quite possible you *don't* need to invest time and attention to finding out whether you ought to be doing this, or finding ways to do it better. *But* it's also possible that you do need to invest that time. One reason is obvious: in recent years, a sharp rise in e-commerce purchases has transformed a lot of business leaders who never thought of their company as being delivery-focused into delivery champions. The landscape has changed because purchasing patterns have changed.

Another reason is that customer *expectations* have changed. These days, anything that saves a trip is likely to factor into a customer's purchasing decisions. That means even companies that don't have products that are traditionally considered "shippable" can save customers time, effort and energy by making delivery part of the service offering. For example, you don't need to go to the salon to get your hair cut if the stylist is willing to "deliver" the service to your home or office.

YOU MAKE THE CALL

Remember, even though I've shared six Convenience Principles with you, in theory you may only need to incorporate one of them to establish a competitive advantage. You must decide which principle or principles make the most sense for growing your business. I'm going to suggest, though, that you look closely at the examples that follow in this section before you rule out delivery – and that you consider whether your industry might be one in which the customer experience could be transformed by bringing the product or service to the customer.

Ten years ago, most big grocery stores didn't "have to" think about delivery. Now, most of them do. Wouldn't you rather be ahead of that kind of curve than behind it?

MOVING BEYOND "MAIL ORDER"

Once upon a time, delivery was called "mail order," and it was typically all about having something delivered to your home in response to a catalogue or an advertisement or a promotion in some form of print media. You clipped out a coupon or order form, filled it out, found a stamp and an envelope, addressed it and sent it off through the post office. Four to six weeks later (doesn't that seem like an awfully long time to wait now?), you received your merchandise. How times have changed! It's easy now to find endless situations in which businesses have used modern communication platforms to make offers that consumers can notice, evaluate and respond to in seconds, with just a few swipes or clicks.

Today's delivery offerings are far faster, as well as more diverse, intuitive, widespread and competitively priced than the ones we read about in the backs of magazines or in catalogues. On every computer screen or smartphone, you're likely to find someone using a digital platform to send or respond to some powerful variation on this enticing message: "Relax. You don't have to come here to buy this. We'll deliver it." By the way, you don't have to be digital to offer delivery. What's happened is that expectations set up in the digital world have forced many other businesses to up their game.

What we used to call "mail order" was always a fringe sector of the economy at best. Today, it's a powerhouse. By incorporating delivery, companies leveraging the contemporary digital approach to marketing, fulfillment and service have radically disrupted, and transformed, the book, grocery and restaurant industries, just to name a few.

THREE POWERFUL ADVANTAGES

The right delivery offering – one that improves the quality of the customer experience – carries three powerful advantages. These three advantages appear to be only rising in importance for today's customers.

- **Save Customers' Time** – You don't have to get in your car or find an alternate means of transport. You don't have to battle crowds as you evaluate different brands and competitive prices. You don't have to deal with long checkout lines. You don't have to visit multiple stores. You don't have to stand there while people work out the administrative details. You get time back in your day that you might not otherwise have.
- **Give Customers More Control Over the Purchase Experience** – You call the shots. If you feel like saving up all your Christmas shopping for the week before

Christmas, you can do that. You may pay a little extra in rush charges – but hey, that's your choice. In many cases, people are willing to pay more for convenience.

- **Save Customers' Attention** – What I mean by that is that delivery gives you one less thing to worry about. Because you're able to wrap up your grocery shopping online (or whatever kind of delivery you're arranging), you're able to move on to something else. You can move on to the next item on your to-do list. You are free to focus on something else. That is a huge advantage.

Add it all up and here's what you get: delivery is worth paying for, and sometimes worth paying a significant premium for. As many companies have learned, their customers are often willing to pay a little extra – or quite a bit extra – for expedited delivery. In these cases, they factor the convenience of delivery into the overall value equation. That means offering a delivery option can sometimes help you compete against price. Typically, the price in these cases doesn't have to be the absolute lowest if it's accompanied by a truly convenient delivery option.

Delivery is all about *removing friction*. That means it is likely to matter in a dramatic way to customers … maybe *your* customers. The right delivery option can be a powerful advantage when it's combined with friendly, knowledgeable people and a good service experience that exceeds expectations. Suddenly, you've created a significant market advantage – and a barrier to your competition.

CONVENIENCE REVOLUTIONARY PROFILE: KIRKWOOD AUDI

"There is always room for those who can be relied upon
to deliver the goods when they say they will."[2]

– NAPOLEON HILL

Reducing friction is a universal principle for distinguishing yourself while disrupting competitors in literally any market. You can find a way to reduce friction for your customers whether you are a big player or a small player in your world; whether you have been around for decades or you've just started your company. In this Convenience Revolution profile, you get an example of a smaller outfit using the Delivery principle to reduce friction and establish a competitive edge. That's important to notice because it's not just global enterprises with huge R&D and marketing budgets that can compete on convenience. It's everybody! I know that from personal experience as an entrepreneur and (as the following story illustrates) as a customer.

Here's what happened: one morning over breakfast, my wife mentioned that my car was nine years old and that it was probably time for me to start thinking about buying a new one. I tend to hold on to cars for a long time, and she was right. We were now dealing with more service and repair issues than we wanted to. My wife said, "You really need to see the new Audi that just came out. It's just a beautiful car."

I said, "Okay, I'll go take a look at it – but you know what

2   https://books.google.ie/books?id=Xc7qgWzp7nQC&pg=PT42&lpg=PT42&dq="There+is+always+ro om+for+those+who+can+be+relied+upon+to+deliver+the+goods+when+they+say+they+will."

I'm going to do? I'm going to go to a different dealership than the one I plan to buy from."

"Why?"

"Because I don't want my salesperson getting excited that I'm looking at a new car and pressuring me to close the deal. I want to stay in the 'just looking' mode and not feel pressured while I look at the car. Going where they don't know me will be easier." She nodded and agreed that that made sense.

That was my plan: to check out the vehicle in a dealership I wasn't all that familiar with, and then go back to the one I had bought my last three cars from and make the purchase there. That's not what happened, though.

At this point I need to explain the reason I liked working with the original dealership that I purchased my cars from: *it was convenient.* They were a little less than a mile away from my office. It was easy to get to. I could drop the car off when it needed repairs, and on a nice day I could walk to work and then walk back to pick it up. That's *less friction* than other dealerships, and that was a primary driver in my decision to do business with them. Of course, if their prices had been dramatically higher than everybody else's, I would have had to stop and re-evaluate. But, their prices were competitive. Not the lowest available, but competitive. So, the convenience was a major factor, and I really didn't have any stronger reason to do business there.

Then I went to Kirkwood Audi, with a location not nearly as convenient, just to see the car.

The salesperson there was very nice when I told him I was just looking. Of course, that's what most people are doing. He answered all my questions and let me take the car out for a test drive, and I realized that my wife was absolutely right. It was an amazing car. I fell in love with it within the first five minutes. I thought to myself, "This is my new car."

I came back and thanked the salesperson for all his help. I believe in being up-front with people, so I told him, "You know what, I love this car, but your dealership is not near where I live. The reason I like to do business with the other dealership is because they're just a mile away from my office. When there's a service issue, I can just drop the car off and walk straight to my office. That's the only reason I'm not talking to you about wrapping this up."

The salesperson smiled and said, "I understand. But before you go, can I ask you a question?"

"Sure," I said.

"Look around you," he said with a sweeping gesture of his arm that took in the whole dealership. "Do you see a big room where customers get to wait with their kids while their car is being serviced?"

I looked around. He was right. There was no such room. I couldn't remember a dealership that didn't give the customer some place to sit and distract the kids while the car was repaired.

"No," I said. "That's strange. Why don't you have one?"

"We actually do have a small waiting room out near the service area. But here's the thing. Most of the time our customers don't have to wait. Unless they bring the car in for something quick or there's an emergency, they don't set foot in the dealership. When you do need service, here's what happens: you make an appointment, we come pick up your car, we make sure you have a loaner car, usually a brand-new Audi, we drop off your car when it's fixed, and we don't charge you a penny extra for that service."

"Really?" I could hardly believe my ears.

"Yes," he said. "In a perfect world, the next time you set foot in this dealership, it will be to buy a new car."

And you know what? That was worth it to me. Their price was competitive. Their service was better. The way they differentiated themselves was by removing friction. Even though they were farther away, they were more convenient than the other dealership. Notice again, that Kirkwood Audi didn't have the rock-bottom lowest price. They just had to have a *competitive* price. And that was enough to tip the scales, given the additional convenience.

You may not be used to thinking of an auto dealership providing a delivery service, but Kirkwood Audi does, and it makes a difference. It's how they do business. Not only did I buy *that* car from them, seven years ago ... I bought my next car (the one my wife now drives) from them, too! So, this is a story of winning a *long-term* customer by thinking creatively about ways to use delivery to reduce the *short-term* friction the customer experiences.

DELIVERY SNAPSHOT: MONOPRIX

Earlier in this book, you read how committed Amazon is to removing friction for its customers, and how doing so is a driving factor in the company's ongoing plans for growth, disruption and dominance in multiple markets. One of those markets is grocery retailing, specifically a brick-and-mortar store concept known as Amazon Go that recently opened in Seattle. Amazon posted a video showing shoppers in the store using the Amazon Go app, and it sent shock waves through the grocery industry. The app senses when a customer has selected a product, notes the section, and charges the customer's account when he or she leaves the store. Translation: no checkout line. Just pick up what you want and walk out of the store.

This prompted the French department and grocery store chain Monoprix to post a video of its own, promoting a service it calls *Monoprix Livraison à domicile +* ("Monoprix Home Delivery +"), which has been popular with customers for more than a decade. Customers who sign up for the program can shop in person, load up their carts, leave them at the front of the store and then head home. Two to three hours later, the groceries show up via courier at the customer's home, at which point the customer pays, although you can also pay at the store if you want.

The Monoprix video even pokes fun at Amazon indirectly, saying (in French): "You don't have to have an app to go shopping. So, put away your phone and shop! It's just that simple." Point taken! You could even argue that the Monoprix service is *more* convenient than the Amazon concept, since it handles the job of getting the delivery home for the shopper. Amazon Go is certainly an exciting option, and Amazon's recent purchase of Whole Foods and its entire grocery delivery system is also part of the mix ... but notice that one of the ways Monoprix has secured an advantage in the marketplace is by making the traditional grocery store experience more convenient.

This cool story does three things. First and foremost, it spotlights a really good delivery idea that a major retailer has successfully implemented to reduce friction for its customers. Second, it shows how a relentless pursuit of convenience can affect customer expectations over time. French customers have come to expect this innovative delivery service; who's to say U.S. customers won't or shouldn't? And third, it shows how humans can create the convenience that others are using automation and technology to create.

For the record, it's worth noting that long before Amazon started testing the waters in the grocery business, Monoprix had a demonstrated commitment to raising the bar in terms of convenience for its customers. It has built up an extremely loyal and vocal fan base in France.

"There is a chain store famous for offering real finds year-round, and at affordable prices: Monoprix. The much beloved chain boasts over 200 locations in France, and is owned by the powerful Casino group. Other Casino stores include giant hypermarkets typically located in the suburbs, or less-than-glamorous but convenient neighborhood supermarkets like Franprix. Most are just stores; and that's why Monoprix is special, and a success story. As a die-hard urbanite, I can only love a store that I can walk to, especially if it offers an irresistible combination of convenience (one-stop shopping) and fun. As I tell my friends before they visit Paris: 'If your hotel or apartment is within walking distance of at least one Metro station and a Monoprix, jackpot!'"

– FRENCH GIRL IN SEATTLE, *Shopping au Monoprix*

DELIVERY SNAPSHOT: USPACK

I mentioned earlier that the subscription service Amazon Prime has started offering customers a delivery option that would once have been unthinkable for a retail operation: free two-hour delivery on certain items.[3] I'm tempted to say that this is likely to remain the gold standard in terms of free delivery, but I've learned that it's never safe to try to write the final word about Amazon's ongoing battle against friction in the customer experience.

Who knows? Maybe in a couple of years, Amazon might figure out a way to get their service all the way down to a free *10-minute* delivery for Amazon Prime members. I wouldn't want to be the one to rule it out. In the meantime, let's consider what an outfit called USPack now offers its local customers in St. Louis, where I live, not as a free service, but as one of the core offerings of its business: *one-hour* expedited courier shipment service within the metropolitan St. Louis area. That delivery timeframe is better than Amazon's. Whenever something like that happens, it's worth noticing.

USPack is a national "last mile" logistics leader that has grown organically and through strategic acquisitions. It offers a wide array of services throughout its local and regional operations centers, such as warehousing, trucking and the above-mentioned one-hour service known as STAT delivery. And yes, customers do pay a premium for this level of service, but that's the point. When someone in St. Louis has a shipment that

---

3   https://www.forbes.com/sites/amitchowdhry/2017/02/21/amazon-free-shipping-order-minimum/#7159bc54d3c2

absolutely, positively, has to be there *within an hour* – not overnight – and they're willing to pay a little more to make sure it arrives intact and on time, USPack is there for them.[4]

POTENT QUOTE

"Same-day delivery services have become a key differentiator for brands hoping to distinguish themselves in a crowded, hyper-competitive market."

– JIM ASHTON, NEWSPRING HOLDINGS

The local USPack operations hub has the tag line "Because Minutes Matter," emphasizing its one-hour service. What I want you to notice about this example is that it shows how local or regional businesses can effectively target customers and establish a strong competitive advantage in the market by creating a more convenient delivery option. By the way, typical customers who take advantage of this option are medical facilities sending drugs and essential equipment to other medical personnel. So in many cases, the convenience USPack offers literally has a life-saving impact.

---

4   http://www.jslogistics.com/Express.aspx

DELIVERY SNAPSHOT: INSOMNIA COOKIES

Here's one of life's great questions: Where can you go if you want to get a hot cookie delivered at 2:00 in the morning?

And here's the great answer: InsomniaCookies.com, that's where. When you need a hot cookie fix after hours and don't feel like driving or using the oven – or maybe *shouldn't* be driving or using the oven, for whatever reason – this is the destination of choice. This company specializes in delivering warm, delicious cookies right to the doors of individuals and companies alike – until 3 a.m. It currently operates in 33 states in the U.S. You can type in a zip code to determine whether an Insomnia outlet is close enough to deliver to you. If not, there's always the online shipping option, which uses FedEx to get you your "cookie fix" the next business day.

Deliveries to local customers take about 40 minutes. The company even offers an online Cookie Tracker that lets you check the status of your order from the moment you place it until it shows up at your door. That's convenient.

There are a number of competitors offering similar services; I picked Insomnia because it has a clear target audience and a great story. The chain was launched in 2003 by college student Seth Berkowitz, who set up an impromptu bakery from his dorm room![5]

The company has since expanded to more than 90 brick-and-mortar locations that make deliveries starting at 10 a.m. and ending at 3 a.m. on weekdays; the deliveries don't start until noon on weekends. This highlights an important point

---

5   http://www.bizjournals.com/philadelphia/news/2013/03/08/another-place-to-get-a-cookie-at-3-in.html

about convenience: What is convenient for one business is unacceptable in other businesses. If my car mechanic didn't open until noon, I would question his business sense. But given Insomnia Cookies' name and branding, it doesn't seem like the store opening at noon is very inconvenient at all.

POTENT QUOTE:

"The fact that Insomnia is open and delivers warm cookies to your door until 3 AM makes it nearly impossible to ignore."

– SPOON UNIVERSITY REVIEW OF INSOMNIA COOKIES

DELIVERY SNAPSHOT: TOM JAMES

Lots of people, when they hear the word "delivery," think of a shipment that arrives via the postal service or a courier like UPS or FedEx. There's nothing wrong with that kind of delivery, of course, but the Tom James Company, which has been making and delivering fine, personally-tailored clothing since 1966, shows how a personal touch and a commitment to quality can take the delivery experience to the level of luxury.

Although you can visit a Tom James location if you want, the company is famous for sending a personal wardrobe stylist to your home or office on your schedule "to help define your style." They don't just measure you for a suit of clothes; they *design* one with you collaboratively.

Tom James doesn't just deliver clothing, although that is the end result. Before it delivers the suit, it delivers a unique, unforgettable experience of working with a fine tailor. Its consultants show up with a briefcase containing fabric samples, visual aids and other tools of the trade. They conduct an in-depth discussion so they can understand what you do, who you interact with, what your professional clothing wardrobe currently looks like, what's working for you right now, and what needs

POTENT QUOTE

"We love Tom James. ... My husband, Chris, looks amazing in their suits and has been a loyal customer for over 16 years. Wendy & Scott are wonderful to work with. ... They supply suits, shirts, socks, ties, belts, shoes, and much more. We traveled to a meeting in California and Chris forgot a tie & belt - she overnighted some things along with collar stays. Thank you, Wendy & Scott, for making my life easy, and my husband looks amazing in your clothes."

- ONLINE REVIEW OF TOM JAMES COMPANY

to be updated or altered. Then your stylist implements what you've chosen. If you like what comes back, you add it to your wardrobe. If you don't, they tweak it until you do. That takes "delivery" way beyond dropping off a jacket, a shirt and a pair of trousers.

These are custom-tailored clothes crafted to match not just your body, but also your style and professional objectives. Make no mistake, this is a luxury experience and it's not inexpensive, but the prices are competitive with other wardrobe services at this level. The big competitive differentiator is that Tom James brings the store – and the personal attention – to you.

DELIVERY SNAPSHOT: 1-800-FLOWERS.COM

This innovative company is totally (and I do mean totally) focused on making the customer's experience easier. Of course, delivery is at the heart of its business model.

It all started back in 1976. Jim McCann was an entrepreneur who owned several flower shops in the New York City area. Ten years later, he acquired the 1-800-Flowers phone number from another company that was going out of business and started promoting the number relentlessly. The rest is history. Notice that the company's historic, brilliant marketing breakthrough removed friction. The phone number was easy – and convenient – to remember. It saved people from having to go to a directory to look up the number for a flower delivery service.

McCann eventually expanded the business from the phone to online, and the company has now become one of the most successful online businesses in the world. 1-800-Flowers.com has not only established a worldwide network of floral delivery shops, but also earned an excellent reputation for its high level of service. It has done this by combining an old-fashioned commitment to making things easier for the customer with innovative thinking and technology.

Delivery may be at the center of its value proposition, but there is even more to this company's convenience strategy. Here are three of its superb best practices for making life easier for customers.

- **Think Outside the Box** – 1-800-Flowers.com figured out a better way to deliver flowers during busy times like Valentine's Day and Mother's Day. A late delivery on Valentine's Day is bad for future business. Angry customers whose orders are not delivered may not give 1-800 Flowers.com a second chance. Recognizing the potential problem during these high-volume times, the company suggested that its network of floral shops use a different delivery system than the traditional and expensive approach of hiring and training temporary staff. It recommended using Lyft and Uber drivers for delivery. This was a win/win, benefiting both the florist and the customer. The florist didn't have to go to the expense of hiring extra employees and the customer had the order delivered on time.
- **Convenient Customer Service Is More Than Just Delivering Flowers (and Other Gifts) on Time** – If your core business is built around delivery, there are bound to be customers who call with questions or complaints about their deliveries. 1-800-Flowers.com has amazing response times for customers who have questions about

their deliveries. Since it is an online business, its customers go online to get issues resolved. That includes its website and social media channels, where 1-800-Flowers.com is a world leader in response times. While studies have shown that the average response time for a customer posting a problem or issue on Facebook is more than three hours, and more than seven hours on Twitter, 1-800-Flowers.com responds in an amazing five minutes![6] That's the foundation of a better, easier customer experience.

- **Expand the Brand and Deliver More, Smoothly** – If 1-800-Flowers.com could deliver flowers, why not deliver other items that tied in well for customers who buy flowers? The company acquired Fannie May for candy and chocolate, Wolferman's for gourmet foods, Harry and David for fruit baskets and specialty gifts, and more. While each of these businesses operates as an individual company, they are still interconnected. 1-800-Flowers.com worked with IBM to create a system that delivers a seamless experience for customers who want to send a gift that combines products from these different brands. That means a customer can order flowers from 1-800-Flowers.com and chocolates from Fannie May in the same order, and if there is a customer service issue, the customer only needs to make one call, even though it's two brands.

The lesson here is simple and powerful: whether you're dealing with multiple brands or multiple departments within a

---

6   https://www.forbes.com/sites/shephyken/2017/02/04/1-800-flowers-has-a-firmly-rooted-culture-of-customer-service/#2b9e1c267fe5

company, make the customer "handoff" experience convenient – preferably invisible. Don't tell the customer those dreaded words, "I'll have to transfer you. That's not my department." That only increases friction.

POTENT QUOTE

"1-800-Flowers.com, the flower provider whose sales grew 2.2 percent to $239.5 million in Q4 2017 from a year earlier, now lets customers order through Google Assistant. ... Shoppers can specify same-day delivery or schedule gift arrival for a future date. A list of gift categories lets on-the-go shoppers select and place orders for flowers and other products for delivery nationwide via voice tech on some Android and iPhone models."

– MOBILE MARKETER

THE TAKEAWAYS

Delivery is all about saving the customer time.

Think back to Kirkwood Audi. I chose to buy from them because once or twice a year they would likely save me two 45-minute trips to and from the service center. Did that make a difference for me? Yes. That's three hours I could be spending with my family. Again, the price was competitive, and all other things being equal, I chose the most convenient option.

Before you rule out a delivery option, consider how likely today's customers are to *expect* to have things delivered. We used to have to stand in line to get concert tickets. Now we buy them online and have them delivered to our phone weeks or months before the event.

Before you move on to the next chapter, give yourself some time to write down answers to the following questions. You may not have an answer for each one, but if you take the time to ponder them, you may discover an answer you hadn't previously considered.

- How much time are your customers currently spending waiting, driving or standing in line for something they get from you? How much time could your customers save if you offered a delivery option?

- If you already offer a delivery option, how do your customers feel about it? Is there any useful feedback about how it could be improved? Are there any consistent customer complaints about your delivery option? If so, what can be done to address these? What delivery options does your competition offer?
- If you provide services and not products, how can you bring your service to the customers?

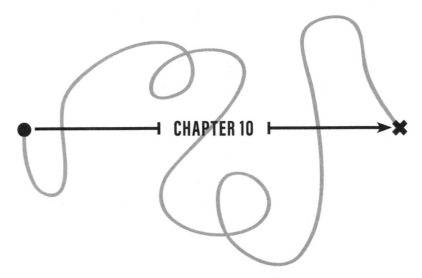

CHAPTER 10

An In-Depth Look at Principle Six: Access

"Today's customers want to be able to get in touch with a company quickly and easily, whether by phone, email or chatting online. The smartest businesses recognize that and make themselves easily available across all channels. ... Clients, quite rightly, expect their queries to be dealt with quickly; and companies who don't are risking the loss of customers and a tarnished reputation."[1]

– JEFF HADEN

---

1   https://www.inc.com/jeff-haden/6-things-customers-really-hate-and-what-great-businesses-do-instead.html

Access simply means going where the customer is. For some companies, access means creating and supporting enough physical locations to serve the target market they've identified in a way that supports convenience. For some companies, access means giving customers user-friendly communication tools through which the customer experience plays out remotely without adding friction. And for some companies, it's going to be essential to do both of those things to provide customers with convenient access.

Only you can decide what's right for your business and what the right balance is going to be. It's important to remember, however, that your customers are always going to have the last word when it comes to deciding whether you really are there for them. They will vote on that with their purchases.

This is one of the easiest Convenience Principles for people to understand for the simple reason that all of us *are* customers who have, at one point or another, been let down by a company that wasn't there for us. The whole point of this Convenience Principle is to keep your customers from feeling that way. You do that by looking closely at three different areas of the customer experience: availability, communication and location.

AVAILABILITY

All of us can remember multiple negative customer experiences we had that were rooted in someone not being available to us when we needed them. Maybe a store we were planning to visit was closed, even though it was supposed to be open; maybe we were waiting a ridiculously long time to get an eye exam; maybe we were waiting on hold to get an answer from tech support. Each of those negative experiences represents a potential opening for a competitor who is willing and able to do a better job of being there for the customer.

First, consider how much time, effort and energy it takes to secure a customer in the first place; and then, how much more diverse, flexible and powerful the available communication tools are than they were just a few years back. And yet, customers still face major problems with availability. All too often we're told that we can only reach the company on the company's terms, at times that make sense for the company, in a way that makes sense to the company. If you doubt this, ask yourself how you as a customer felt about the "availability" of a utility company that made you call them during your work hours to address a pressing issue ... and then made you wait on hold for an extended period before you could talk to someone who may or may not have been qualified to deal with your issue. That's low availability. Customers hate it, and they have a right to.

COMMUNICATION

In the area of *communication,* customers want a simple, direct, respectful exchange that gets them measurably closer to what they're after in real time. They don't want to be put on hold. They don't want to wait in line. They don't want to have to explain the same issue multiple times to multiple team members. They don't want to get different answers from multiple departments. Ideally, they want a straight answer, now, without doubletalk or delay. If they don't get that, they're not getting the access they crave.

What they get instead, in a lot of cases, is hassle: hold music, a transfer to another line, a suggestion that they go somewhere else – anywhere else, an abrupt, mechanized order from the company to fill out some kind of online application – such as the dreaded "service ticket." These are classic examples of friction, something most of us will go out of our way to *avoid* if we possibly can. This kind of hassle can happen in person or online.

Whenever friction shuts down communication, access suffers. Here's an example of what I mean. A friend of mine was shopping at one of the big retailers (I won't say which) during the holiday season. He asked where he could find a certain flat-screen TV that was on sale. He was directed to the far end of the store, which had nothing whatsoever to do with electronics as it turned out. He made the long walk back to the person he'd asked for help, who then flat-out admitted that he'd sent my friend to the wrong part of the store because he didn't feel like explaining that the model in question was sold out.

That's the exact opposite of being there for your customer. Who cares if you're open at all hours if the customer can't get an answer from you that reflects reality?

LOCATION

With regard to *location,* customers want to be able to connect with us at a time and place that matches up seamlessly with everything else that's going on in their busy day. Because we live in the 21st century, *location* can mean two things: a physical place where the customer shows up in person or a fully-resourced Internet presence that gives the customer a similar or even better experience online. Those can each be expressions of good location from the customer's point of view.

By the way, you might not think of a physical store that's too crowded to serve its customers well as a failure of location, but there are plenty of successful businesses that have realized that's exactly what it is. You'll learn more about that critical distinction in this chapter.

What good location *doesn't* look like is what customers too often have to deal with: physical outlets that are jammed or are only open during the times when they are busy doing something else, and websites that claim to offer 24/7 service, but really don't because there's no one there to respond when the customer poses a question after hours. ("Thanks for visiting our website. If you have a problem or issue, please leave a comment using this form and we'll be back in touch eventually, if we're not too busy.")

When we give customers less than they have a right to expect in terms of *availability, communication* and/or *location*, we are adding friction to their already friction-heavy day, and we are opening a door to our competition.

Please understand, I'm not saying you have to offer the same level of Access that a globally dominant player like Amazon does. What I am saying is that you should take the time to figure out specifically which customers you are targeting and serving; what level of access in each of these three areas they should expect to receive from you, given all the time, effort and expense you have dedicated to getting them to buy from you in the first place; and finally, what the competition is likely to do in terms of improving the level of Access that customers get in your industry. Once you've done that, you can make the right decision for your business.

CONVENIENCE REVOLUTIONARY PROFILE: HUNTINGTON BANK

"Got to be there."

— CLASSIC POP LYRIC BY ELLIOT WILLENSKY FROM THE SONG OF THE SAME NAME

A good friend of mine lives in Ireland, where the phrase "bankers' hours" hasn't lost any of its real-life impact – or its potential to remind customers of problems they'd rather not have to deal with. On most working days, banks in Ireland don't open until 10 a.m., and they close by 4 p.m. So, if you live in Ireland, and you work 9-to-5 hours, your lunch hour may be the only time you can visit the bank. So, you skip your meal and head to the branch, which you're likely to find jammed with people who are just as hungry, stressed and eager to get back to work as you are.

Bankers' hours are a classic example of friction.

From the middle of the 19th century all the way up until the mid-1960s, the friction was even worse in the United States with most banks opening around 10 a.m. and closing around 3 p.m., much to the disappointment and inconvenience of their customers. No wonder people started muttering disapprovingly under their breaths about "bankers' hours." That phrase became famous – or infamous, depending on how you look at it – because it illustrated a core truth: *the hours in question are convenient for the bankers, not for their customers.*

Unfortunately for customers, that's still how many banks operate. Many American banks operate on a 9-to-5 weekday schedule with no weekend hours, which means that it's only ntly easier for customers with busy schedules to get face time with banking personnel in Dublin, California, than it would be in Dublin, Ireland.

Of course, it's true that ATMs, mobile apps, call centers and online web portals now give customers access to many banking services and resources that once had to be obtained in person. And that's great. Still, there are plenty of times when customers need to discuss financial matters in person with a bank representative.

This chapter is all about access. As you'll recall, I've defined providing access to your customer as *deciding where your market is, and then making sure you're there.* Columbus, Ohio-based Huntington Bank leads this section because it has made a strategic decision to reduce friction for its customers in the North Central and Mid-Atlantic regions by broadening access in a way that many of its competitors don't. Huntington makes it much easier for busy customers to drop in at a convenient time to discuss banking issues in person. That shouldn't be a revolutionary idea, but in this industry it is.

Huntington Bank has secured a significant competitive advantage in the marketplace by expanding customers' personal access to its employees, both in person and via a toll-free phone call. Banking is one of those industries that can have a huge impact on our quality of life, without us ever getting a sense of personal interaction with the *people* at the bank who are delivering the service. Although the "personal touch" is incredibly important, most banks don't seem to make it much of a priority. In some cases, the technology they offer becomes more of a wall than a bridge.

Yes, it's certainly convenient to be able to make a deposit at

an ATM at 2:00 in the morning, or to get a simple loan decision online quickly. Very often, though, when we need personal
help and guidance with an important issue that connects to our
finances, we want a little more than technology has to offer. We
don't want to be told to visit a website or send an email. We
want to be able to look someone in the eye. That's only natural
if we're talking about something as important as the purchase
of a home, or whether our child is going to be able to afford to
go to the college he or she wants to go to.

Huntington Bank's management has figured out that these
discussions truly matter to customers on a personal level. It has
decided that supporting such moments is a strategic imperative. It has opted to show a little more creativity than the competition when scheduling its hours of operation.

No surprise, then, that *Money* magazine recently named
Huntington as the bank with the best hours in the United
States. Its brick-and-mortar facilities are typically open 68
hours a week, including 13 hours on Saturday and Sunday. As
if that weren't enough, Huntington's policy is to open its doors
10 minutes earlier and close 10 minutes later than the official
posted hours, just for the convenience of its customers.

Brick-and-mortar isn't its entire customer experience, of
course. In keeping with the idea of *deciding where your market
is, and then making sure you're there,* Huntington also has a
highly rated website that scores well with both consumers and
industry analysts. Its mobile apps earn strong marks from users,
and the bank offers well-reviewed online banking features
that today's customers have come to expect, such as automatic
bill pay and online statements. The bank's customer service

infrastructure is impressive, with a state-of-the-art 24/7 phone help line; and, if there's a long wait, the auto-attendant tells you about how long you're likely to be on hold, and gives you the option to stay on the line or hang up and have a Huntington customer service rep call you directly. There's even a Twitter feed, @AskHuntington, which does a great job of answering customer queries.

Put it all together and you have a powerful, coordinated experience built around Access, a Convenience Principle that does a great job, in person and remotely, of removing unnecessary friction from the typical customer's day. Not surprisingly, the consumer response has been strong and constitutes a major market advantage.

As of this writing, Huntington was the *only* regional bank to have claimed the top ranking in J.D. Power's U.S. Retail Banking Satisfaction Study in more than one part of the country, taking top honors in both the North Central and Mid-Atlantic regions. That's quite an accomplishment. And Steve Steinour, Chairman, President and CEO of Huntington, attributed the strong customer response to a long-term strategic choice. "Positive feedback from our customers," he said, "resulting in J.D. Power recognition, is validation that our customer-first strategy continues to work and is the right way to do business."

What Steinour calls a "customer-first strategy" is precisely the same thing I've referred to throughout this book as "reducing friction," and it's what has driven the bank not only to offer some of the best personal access in the industry, but also to create innovative policies that are sufficiently exciting for customers to tell their friends and family members about them. Heading the list here is something called 24-Hour Grace, which is a free component of all the bank's checking and money market accounts. Under 24-Hour Grace, if your account drops below zero, you have until midnight of the next business day to get you balance back up and avoid the fee. Here's the part I love: you don't even have to get it up to the zero mark. The service kicks in if you bring your balance up to at least negative five dollars.

Huntington's extended hours of operation are the kind of customer-focused strategy that makes customers ask, "Hey, why aren't other banks offering that?" My prediction is that

> POTENT QUOTE:
>
> ___
>
> *"The staff is always friendly and smiles at me each time I see them. The service is quick and professional. ... (Sometimes) the ATM does not like certain bills or certain conditions of money. It is just a few steps to a friendly teller who makes my deposit with a smile and quick service. ... I have had many hassles with my old bank, but never with this one. Thank you for being great, Huntington!"*
>
> — ONLINE CUSTOMER REVIEW OF HUNTINGTON BANK

they will. Why? Because banks, and many other types of businesses, know that when they go out of their way to find seemingly simple, and sometimes innovative, ways to remove friction from the customer experience, they will raise the bar and set new standards for everyone else.

ACCESS SNAPSHOT: ENTERPRISE RENT-A-CAR

Given Enterprise's now-legendary tag line, "We'll pick you up," you might have expected that I would place this entry in the Delivery section, since picking up a rental car customer means getting that customer *to* the car, which is basically the same as delivering the car. But focusing on delivery would have missed the point. What Enterprise has really been saying for more than two decades with that famous slogan is something far bigger, something that has always been part of its strategy and part of its corporate culture: Enterprise goes where the customers are.

Enterprise Rent-A-Car's primary market has been customers who needed a replacement car as the result of an accident, mechanical problem, stolen vehicle or an event such as a vacation or a business trip. What sets it apart is its commitment to *make renting a car easier for customers, no matter where t* *might happen to be.* Yes, it has airport locations, but that i what made Enterprise the largest rental car company in world. It was the fact that they were willing to go where ot rental car companies often wouldn't, including car dealersl and other nontraditional locations. That's where the "We'll you up" promises applies – by the way – at those thousand *non*-airport locations, which are the overwhelming majorit its outlets.

POTENT QUOTE
———

"I have traveled a ton over the course of both my professional and personal life. I've dealt with numerous rental car agencies. I had never dealt with Enterprise, but selected them because of their proximity to my home. It is ultra-convenient!"

– ONLINE REVIEW OF ENTERPRISE RENT-A-CAR

Expanding customer access to convenient auto transport is the way this company has done business since its founding in 1957. The company now has more than 5,000 offices located within 15 miles of 90 percent of the U.S. population, as well as hundreds of overseas locations.[2] That extraordinary reach enables Enterprise to operate not only for insurance replacement, weekend getaway and special occasion customers, but also as a viable local transportation alternative for other underserved markets. One innovative new approach the company has taken to give its customers greater access is an app-driven *hourly* rental and car-sharing service targeting select metropolitan areas.[3] Wow!

---

2   https://www.enterpriseholdings.com/en/press-archive/2016/02/enterprise-rent-a-car-reports-slight-rise-in-fourth-quarter-2015-length-of-rental-data.html
3   https://www.enterprisecarshare.com/us/en/home.html

ACCESS SNAPSHOT: WALMART

I hope you'll recall that the powerful convenience strategy I've identified as Access can be defined as "knowing where your market is – and then going there." Having thought about this aspect of convenience for a good long while, I'm having a hard time coming up with any companies in any industry that have done a better job of providing access than Amazon and Walmart.

It's ironic that Amazon is now moving into brick-and-mortar retail, while Walmart is busily strengthening its online platforms. You can expect an ongoing battle between these two titans to develop more and more convenient options for retail customers in the years ahead.

Of course, you've already read in the earlier chapters about Amazon's commitment to Access – to being there for its customers on their timeline, at their pace and via a platform that makes sense to them. Now consider the following facts about Walmart, the world's largest company by revenue[4] ... and take a moment to consider how the company's extraordinary success matches up to its willingness to invest in strategically expanding the Access it offers to customers.

90 percent of all U.S. residents live within 10 minutes of a Walmart.[5]

Every week, one-third of the U.S. population visits a Walmart store.[6]

---

4   http://fortune.com/global500/walmart/
5   http://www.businessinsider.com/16-walmart-facts?op=1/#is-year-everyone-in-the-world-will-make-an-average-of-11-purchases-at-a-walmart-3
6   http://www.businessinsider.com/16-walmart-facts?op=1/#is-year-everyone-in-the-world-will-make-an-average-of-11-purchases-at-a-walmart-3

Online purchases at Walmart.com – an intuitive, user-friendly platform that just won Sitejabber's Customer Choice Award for Best Online Discount Shopping Site – were up 29 percent in the most recent year, which means Walmart's online revenues are rising at a faster rate than Amazon's![7]

One of the most popular options at Walmart.com is Store Pickup, which allows customers to skip the crowds and the physical navigation of the store, place their orders online, and then pick up their order at the store at a time that's convenient. No shipping or delivery charge. (Perishable items and some other products are not eligible for this service … but read on.)

The online Walmart Grocery option allows Walmart customers to order grocery items via Grocery.Walmart.com, then drive to the store, where Walmart employees provide curbside delivery service. Again, no shipping or delivery charge.

From the beginning, Walmart's development strategy has been built around the concept of each Walmart store being within easy driving distance of another Walmart store.[8] This means lower delivery and logistical expenses, which keeps prices down, but it also means that any given Walmart customer always has a couple of stores to choose from (and point friends and relatives toward). This built-in geographical convenience is an under-reported part of the Walmart success story.

Most of us, when we think of the reasons for Walmart's market dominance, think of two things: low prices and huge selection. That's an extraordinary combination to be sure, but it makes sense to work something else into the conversation: Access.

---

7   http://money.cnn.com/2017/02/21/investing/walmart-earnings-amazon/index.html
8   https://www.minneapolisfed.org/publications/fedgazette/thomas-j-holmes-on-walmarts-location-strategy

---

POTENT QUOTE

"According to a recent study, 90 percent of Americans live within 15 miles of a Walmart - and thank goodness, that includes me. I am about 4 miles from our Super Walmart and I am thrilled about that! I can go there whenever I need something and not have to drive very far. Plus, it's very close to a lot of other retail stores, so it's even more convenient."

— ONLINE REVIEW OF WALMART

ACCESS SNAPSHOT: ANYTIME FITNESS

How do you make your gym automatically stand out from every other gym in town? Make it more accessible than the competition. That's what Anytime Fitness has done, and it's one of the hottest franchises in America.[9]

As the name implies, every Anytime Fitness location is open 24 hours a day, 365 days a year. That means that if you feel like working out on Christmas Day or in the middle of the night or in the hour before you start your regular working day, you can

---

9   https://www.prnewswire.com/news-releases/anytime-fitness-named-1-top-global-franchise-by-entrepreneur-magazine-300105008.html

head over to Anytime and get your heart pumping on a schedule that works for you.

The franchise chain boasts more than 4,000 gym locations and 3 million members, who use a computerized key system to get secure access to gym facilities, even during unstaffed hours. Reliable access to club facilities during unstaffed hours is the foundation of the chain's 24-hour convenience, a powerful and memorable brand promise in every market where it operates.

If you're the owner of a local franchise, maybe you're wondering how to make sure your gym location is being used properly when there's no staff on site. Simple. You sign on with ProVision Security – an ancillary business – which is the "exclusive provider of security, surveillance and access control systems for the Anytime Fitness franchise." ProVision brings state-of-the-art surveillance and site control capability to each fitness club location it services. The system gives gym owners

---

POTENT QUOTE

"I love working out here! This is my favorite gym ... by far the cleanest, friendliest and most convenient gym around!"

– ONLINE REVIEW OF ANYTIME FITNESS

peace of mind during off hours and keeps users safe. It's a great business model.

I should note here that Anytime is by no means the only gym providing 24/7 access; however, by all indications it is the biggest and the most successful with rave reviews from customers in all 50 states and in 30 countries. In addition to its convenience, the gym chain wins high marks from customers for its service, cleanliness and commitment to modern technology and workout equipment. *Entrepreneur* magazine has ranked Anytime Fitness No. 1 on its list of Best Franchise Opportunities for three consecutive years.[10] [11]

ACCESS SNAPSHOT: STARBUCKS

If you ever happen to find yourself on the corner of Shepherd and West Gray at the River Oaks Shopping Center in Houston, Texas, you will be able to take your pick from not one, not two, but *three* Starbucks coffee shops located within a block of where you stand. This state of affairs drew the attention of the local news media.[12] The *Houston Chronicle* reported one man's confused response: "There on one corner was a Starbucks. Across the street in the exact same building was another Starbucks. I looked back and forth thinking the sun was playing tricks on my eyes." The story quickly became part of an ongoing national and global discussion that has been playing out for years, with this question at its center: *Why are there so many Starbucks stores located so close to another Starbucks?*

---

10   https://www.entrepreneur.com/article/230291
11   https://www.entrepreneur.com/article/247038
12   http://www.chron.com/business/article/One-on-corner-there-are-3-places-to-get-your-1745816.php

As it turns out, the answer is: *because Starbucks planned it that way.* The company, which analysts project could have 50,000 locations by the year 2021,[13] boasts a nuanced, convenience-focused approach to site selection. The goal is to reduce lines and waiting times for the customer. In other words, Starbucks places a lot of stores in certain carefully targeted, high-traffic city locations to improve the level of Access it offers its legions of coffee-sipping fans. It's not the only company to follow such a strategy; places like McDonald's and Subway do too. Either of those firms could have been profiled here. I chose Starbucks because the chain's extreme visibility in urban markets has already become a hot topic of discussion.

Here's what that means in practical terms: If you're in one of the urban areas the company dominates and you're thinking about getting a latte, there's always going to be a Starbucks nearby, and there's always going to be another one near that. This is so you can get in and out without difficulty, or stick around, without a lot of hassle. The point is, Starbucks wants you to be able to get what you want, when you want it, with as little friction as possible. It doesn't want the store to be so crowded it turns you off.

One of the major ways this massive coffee chain differentiates itself is by offering a pleasant environment for coffee drinkers to just sit and pass the time – whether they're chatting with someone, reading, working or sipping coffee. Founder Howard Schultz has called this the company's "third place"[14] approach.

---

13   https://www.bloomberg.com/news/articles/2017-01-03/starbucks-to-top-mcdonald-s-as-restaurant-king-analyst-predicts
14   https://www.fastcompany.com/887990/starbucks-third-place-and-creating-ultimate-customer-experience

"Starbucks' real estate choices are, in their words, 'as much an art as a science.' When deciding where to hang its next shingle, the company marries right-brain ingenuity with hard-headed, left-brain analysis – exactly as you should."

– SPENCER RASCOFF and STAN HUMPHRIES, writing in *Quartz*

He wants you to think of Starbucks as a place where you *belong* and can spend some significant time … just like your home and your workplace.

As it happens, that business plan has been so successful that in some parts of the country, Starbucks has had to expand its location map dramatically to support the experience its stores are designed to deliver. The profusion of Starbucks outlets in some places may make for a funny newspaper story or an interesting YouTube video, but it also reflects a commitment to Access that is hard to find elsewhere.

ACCESS SNAPSHOT: MOBY MART

Wheelys, a high-concept retail venture based in Sweden, has designed what may turn out to be the most innovative approach to expanding customer access that the retail industry has ever seen. It's Moby Mart, a solar-powered mobile convenience store that navigates multiple locations during the course of a day. You use a special app to place your order and the store comes to you, so you can pick up the merchandise that you ordered online. And there's no human attendant.

Wow!

Moby Mart, "the world's first autonomous, staff-less and mobile store,"[15] is basically a vast, rolling vending machine you can walk right into and explore. It looks a little bit like a futuristic bus or light rail train. The store has custom-designed software that tracks its inventory and alerts the Moby Mart when it's time to restock, so it can take a trip to the warehouse. Wheelys says drones can be deployed from the top of the store to deliver larger items. The whole stunning concept takes Amazon Go – a brick-and-mortar retail store without human staff, now open in Seattle – and raises it to the next level.

"Mobile stores are much more efficient than physical ones," says Wheelys cofounder Per Cromwell. "Mobile stores can serve business areas during the day and residential areas during evenings and weekends. They can also serve the countryside or vacation areas in a smarter way."[16]

The company's website argues that the three biggest costs in retail are staff, rent and restocking. The big idea behind Moby Mart is to dramatically reduce all three budget lines and simultaneously raise the Access bar with a low-friction, high-tech,

15   https://www.themobymart.com/about
16   https://www.dezeen.com/2017/06/28/wheelys-self-driving-moby-mart-grocery-store-holographic-shop-assistant-design-technology/

24/7 retail experience that engages 21st century customers. Talk about disruption!

Wheelys calls the experience "autonomous shopping" and the positive buzz around the idea has been strong and appears to be intensifying. If Uncle Johnny started the modern Convenience Revolution in Dallas back in the 1920s by offering his ice customers eggs, milk and bread, Moby Mart may be positioning itself to continue that revolution nearly a century later by shaking up the retail industry in an equally memorable way, by literally going where the customers are.

The Moby Mart prototype is currently being beta-tested in Shanghai; only time will tell how successful the venture will

---

POTENT QUOTE

"'The Moby Mart offers products for immediate consumption, such as milk, lunch or medicine over the counter, around the clock,' its creators say. 'Just enter the store, take what you need and leave.' The (store) is currently moved around by humans, but the creators say future versions will use computer vision to navigate the streets and come to customers."

– MATT BURGESS in *WIRED*

be on a large scale. I suspect the future of Moby Mart will be closely tied to the future of self-driving and remotely piloted vehicles, which as of this writing are not yet legal on public roads. Even so, there are a lot of *private* roads out there, and the fusion of "autonomous car" technology with online shopping and inventory management technology has created in Moby Mart an exciting and potentially revolutionary retail model that dramatically expands Access.

Stay tuned. Whether or not Moby Mart proves that mobile stores are the wave of the future, it definitely proves one thing: the Convenience Revolution is never over.

THE TAKEAWAYS

Access means being there for your customer. And being there for your customer means giving them what they want and expect in the areas of *availability, communication* and *location*.

Customer expectations in this area are likely to change over time, based on the access they've come to expect in their dealings with other companies. That's one of the remarkable things about the Convenience Revolution: it's constantly raising expectations in the area of Access. People no longer compare you just to your direct competitors. They compare you to the positive experiences they've had with companies in any industry.

Recall the story of 7-Eleven, which invented the modern convenience store back in the 1920s. The store's name reflected management's decision – unheard of at the time – to open its doors to customers at 7:00 in the morning, and stay open until 11:00 at night. They've kept that name, of course, but the expectations have changed a great deal in the decades since. Today's consumers expect a convenience store to be open *24* hours a day. And that's the level of access 7-Eleven gives them.

Before you move on to the next chapter, give yourself some time to write down answers to the

following questions. You may not have an answer for each one, but if you take the time to ponder them, you may discover an answer you hadn't previously considered.

- Are you there for your customers? Specifically, are people available to talk to when they're needed? Is your communication simple, direct and respectful, and does it move the customer forward toward what he or she wants?

- Is your location easy to get to and easy to navigate without waiting too long? What do you do differently from the competition in terms of availability, location and access? How do you offer flexible hours or alternative access during your off hours?

- Where are your customers currently going for what you offer and how do you meet them there?

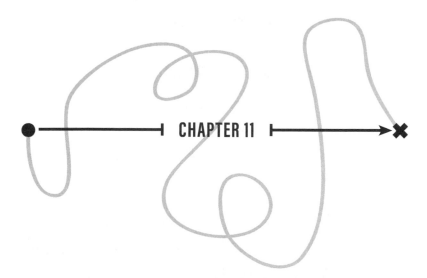

When Does It *Not* Make Sense to Offer More Convenience?

I n this book, we've studied many examples of companies that have leveraged convenience for customers in ways that helped them secure a competitive advantage. We've looked at a lot of cool ideas that show how convenience can be a disruptive force in any marketplace. And we've seen how markets can change quickly based on rising customer expectations for convenience, fueled by interactions with companies like Amazon and Google.

But one thing we haven't yet done is look closely at when it *doesn't* make sense for your company to invest in raising the convenience bar. I want to examine that issue now.

MOVING FROM THE LONG LIST TO THE SHORT LIST

Please don't treat the examples I've offered in the book as a kind of checklist; don't assume that it makes sense to try to implement every single one of the ideas I've shared with you. But please *do* use this book to start brainstorming.

The six principles of convenience we've been talking about – Reducing Friction, Self-Service, Technology, Subscription, Delivery and Access – each represent a huge area of opportunity for you to consider. So, do some creative thinking. Using these categories and the examples within them that are most relevant to your world as starting points, create a "long list" of all the things your company *could* do to make life easier for your customers. Remember: If you don't find a way to distinguish yourself in at least one of these areas, there's a good chance that one of your competitors will!

What do you do with that long list of convenience initiatives? The same thing you do with any long list. You whittle it down to a short list.

As you evaluate all the ideas you've come up with, and shorten the list, you will want to bear in mind that there's a certain point when the idea might sound good to you, but will it be noticed by the customer? I'm all for convenience creating a better customer experience, even if it doesn't disrupt your competitor or your industry. Sometimes it's just the right thing to do for the customer, but the customer should be able to notice. If you run a hotel and you pay extra to have all the rooms equipped with DVD players, but your guests aren't using them to play DVDs, that's not adding convenience.

THE CONVENIENCE REALITY CHECK

This discussion brings us to the question of long-term business planning. Here again, Amazon is an example worth studying. The leadership there has consistently chosen low margins in order to build enduring market share and destabilize competitors in those areas where it has chosen to compete. Not only that, it has consistently reinvested a portion of its massive earnings in processes that make life easier for the customer. Taken together, those two long-term commitments have made it a behemoth and, not coincidentally, the single most convenient company on earth. But there is a third aspect to Amazon's strategy that sometimes goes unnoticed, and is deeply relevant to the testing of new convenience initiatives. I call it the Convenience Reality Check.

This is the point at which, having experimented and tested a certain idea that could deliver its customers greater convenience, and having monitored that idea over time, Amazon's leadership poses a critical question: *Do we shut this initiative down or scale it up?*[1]

That's a great question, not just for Amazon, but for you, too. It's part of the culture at Amazon, part of the operating philosophy that has enabled the company to disrupt multiple markets and leapfrog over multiple competitors. So, make sure you ask that same question. Do you shut the initiative down or scale it up?

Look at that operating philosophy again. It's worth remembering!

---

1   http://uk.businessinsider.com/amazons-biggest-flops-2015-10?r=US&IR=T

- Amazon has consistently chosen lower margins in favor of higher market share.
- Amazon has invested heavily and long-term in processes that make life easier for the customer.
- Amazon has built in "reality check" moments as an integral part of its planning process. Its leadership continually asks, *"Do we shut this initiative down or scale it up?"*

That third element – the "reality check" moment – is the one I want to emphasize now. I urge you to build it into your planning process. It's okay to make a mistake, but it's not okay to keep *funding* a mistake once it's obvious.

Let me explain why this "reality check" is so important. We're used to thinking about Amazon's marketplace triumphs, many of which I've discussed in this book: Amazon Prime, the Kindle, the Echo, and so on. The list of successes, we know, is a long one. These are amazing achievements that secured a competitive advantage by delivering on the promise of greater convenience for the customer. We *should* study them. But in celebrating those successes and learning from them, we must make sure we don't lose sight of the many ideas Amazon chose – wisely – to shut down or scale back dramatically, after testing them and discovering that they simply didn't resonate with the customer or deliver sufficiently on their investment.

Some of the many Amazon bets that didn't pass the "reality check" moment include:

- Amazon Webstore, an e-commerce solution for online stores;
- Amazon Destinations, a hotel booking site;

- Endless.com, a high-end fashion commerce site;
- the Amazon Fire smartphone;
- and WebPay, a solution designed to directly compete with PayPal.

All these failures were learning experiences, and all reflect a willingness to fail. Yes, I realize Amazon's deep pockets allow it to experiment and innovate at a very high level. We may envy those deep pockets, but what we really need to notice is how careful Amazon was to make sure none of its failures sank the company. As Jeff Bezos put it:

I've made billions of dollars of failures at Amazon.com. ... None of those things are fun. But they also don't matter. What really matters is, companies that don't continue to experiment, companies that don't embrace failure, they eventually get in a desperate position where the only thing they can do is a Hail Mary bet at the very end of their corporate existence. Companies that are making bets all along, even big bets — but not bet-the-company bets — prevail. I don't believe in bet-the-company bets. That's when you're desperate. That's the last thing you can do.[2]

This willingness to place a series of intelligent bets on convenience that sometimes fail is what makes success possible. As you test and evaluate new convenience possibilities, you'll have your share of learning experiences, too. That's as it should

2   http://uk.businessinsider.com/amazons-biggest-flops-2015-10?r=US&IR=T/#what-really-matters-is-companies-that-dont-continue-to-experiment-companies-that-dont-embrace-failure-they-eventually-get-in-a-desperate-position-where-the-only-thing-they-can-do-is-a-hail-mary-bet-at-the-very-end-of-their-corporate-existence-bezos-said-2

be. You *should* learn from your failures, just as Jeff Bezos has learned from his.

My advice to you now, as this main part of the book closes, is simple: follow Amazon's example. In distinguishing yourself from the competition, whether that competition is across the street or across the globe, be ready, willing and able to place a bet on convenience for the benefit of your customers. At the same time, I want you to monitor the results. Make sure that the bet you're making really is a smart bet; make sure it's improving your relationships with your best customers; and be honest with yourself about when it's time to step away and focus on something else that better reduces hassle and effort in your customer's world.

As you and your company pick your battles in the ongoing, never-ending Convenience Revolution, I urge you to think big – but also to leave yourself time and space for a "reality check" moment. Test your biggest, best ideas. Experiment. Make smart investments. Figure out when it's time to scale something up. Figure out when it's time to shut something down. And consider reinvesting some of your profit back into refining the customer experience, an experience that reduces friction and creates convenience for your customers. They'll remember. They'll tell others. They'll come back. They'll spend more when they do. That seems like a bet worth placing.

POTENT QUOTE

"The key to mitigating disloyalty is reducing customer effort."

— MATTHEW DIXON, author of *The Effortless Experience: Conquering the New Battleground for Customer Loyalty*

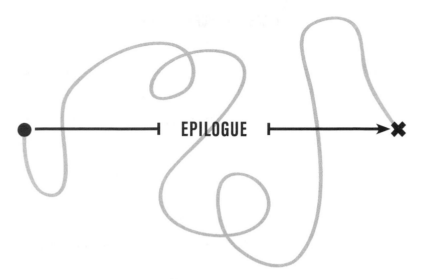

Convenience Is Not Just for Companies

We've spent a lot of time looking at how *companies* can reduce friction, but what about individuals? How can a single person make life more convenient, make things easier, get things to go a little more smoothly for both *external* and *internal* customers? That's a question that every individual within the company must be ready, willing and able to ask. It's not just for company leaders.

Let's take a moment to define our terms here. Most of us have no problem at all visualizing an external customer: it's someone who pays money to receive our company's products or services. But I find there's a lot less familiarity with the concept of the internal customer. An internal customer is anyone within an organization who is dependent on anyone else within the organization. This person may not always be your internal customer. He or she might only be depending on you at a specific time for a specific reason – maybe once a week or even once a year.

Ultimately, everybody supports everybody else in the organization, and we all have a personal obligation to look for ways to raise the convenience bar, no matter what we do or who we report to. Think about it: a company with a reputation for making things convenient for customers didn't earn that reputation without making "attention to convenience" part of the culture. And even if you are not in direct contact and supporting the outside customer, you may be working with someone who is. That means everyone within the organization has an effect, directly or indirectly, on the level of convenience the external customer experiences.

In the most competitive companies, convenience becomes a mindset, an integral part of the culture, and a way of doing business. People at all levels constantly ask themselves, "Am I making it as easy as possible to work with or do business with me? Are there any roadblocks that I can remove? Is there anything that would irritate me or add friction to my day that I might be doing to my colleagues or customers? If so, how could I change that?"

With those questions in mind, consider the following simple list of ways that we, as individuals, can raise the convenience bar in our own world ... no matter what our job title might be or where we may happen to work in the organization.

APPOINT A BACKUP

This one is simple and incredibly easy to do. When you're taking a day off, or are called away from work at any time that you know someone is likely to need you, instead of just leaving a blank space in your world, designate someone who's responsible for fielding your calls or answering inquiries on your behalf. This is a classic friction-reducer you can carry out in a matter of minutes by means of a conversation with a colleague and a few adjustments to your company's phone system and your own email account's "autoresponder" function.

This is an important conversation to have with specific individuals you know will be counting on you while you're out. Here's an example of what I mean. Not long ago, I was working with a printer on a major job that had a tight deadline. My primary contact, Kay, mentioned that she was about to go on vacation the following week. My stomach started to churn – who would handle this print job for me? What would happen if there were problems? I'd come to count on Kay.

But Kay knew what I was thinking. She said, "Shep, don't worry. My colleague Amy has been briefed and knows about the project. She's covering this while I'm on vacation, and she knows exactly what to do. Any emails you send or calls you make will go straight to Amy, and she'll take great care of you." That's exactly what happened – and Amy did a great job. Instead of simply vanishing, or sending me an email telling me that Amy was now in charge, Kay let me know ahead of time and executed a perfect handoff. Bravo!

GO TO WHERE THEY ARE

This means: when you need me, I go to you. I don't make you come to me. I find a way to bring my resources, my skills and my experience to whatever physical location you're at and saying, "How can I help? What do you need from me?" Of course, we can't always deliver that level of service for everyone we might want to. And by the same token, we don't want to fall into the trap of assuming everybody needs to physically come to us whenever there's something to discuss.

Not long ago, a client asked me for a face-to-face meeting at his location. Because it was a fairly small client, my initial instinct was to suggest that we have a videoconference instead. But something inside told me, "Go on and meet with him at his office." I was glad I did. That one in-person meeting led to a referral that turned into a major new piece of business! The personal touch is powerful. It's something you can and should be willing to leverage strategically in your interactions with both internal and external customers.

CALL THEM BEFORE THEY CALL YOU

Whether you're looking at a potential problem or a new opportunity, take the initiative to reach out to the people who are counting on you. Don't put the onus on them to call you.

For instance, if you're in financial services this could mean calling your most important clients to say something like, "You're probably going to be seeing something in the news about XYZ Company, which could affect your investment portfolio. I just wanted you to know that I'm tracking this closely, and I don't see any real problem on the horizon for you, but if that changes, I will definitely be in touch."

If you're experiencing problems with a project deadline, you might call your supervisor before there's a crisis and say, "I'm looking at some late deliverables from a couple of key contributors on the ABC project; I've spent a lot of time renegotiating the due dates with all the team members, and my best estimate now is that we are looking at November 7 as the wrap-up date, rather than October 20. I felt sure you'd want to know. I'll keep you posted each week on how that's looking as we move forward."

Let's face it, problems and delays happen. They're part of our working life. In some instances, you may not be able to eliminate friction, but you can at least reduce it – and improve the quality of the working relationship – by reaching out first and showing that you're on top of the situation.

ASK HOW YOU CAN MAKE WORKING WITH YOU EASIER

When you wrap up a task for someone who counts on you and/ or your team, why not take a moment to ask how it went? Why not ask, "Hey, how easy were we to work with?" In fact, why not ask them to rate you on a scale of one to 10 to let you know how hassle-free the experience of working with you or buying from you was? If you get any score less than a 10, then ask, "What would I need to do to get that up to a 10?"

The most competitive teams and organizations are constantly asking questions like these and measuring their performance. If you don't ask, you won't know what you need to do to improve the level of convenience you deliver.

MAKE IT AUTOMATIC

A while back, I did a speech for a client. After the speech, the client called me up and said, "We saw a big difference at the event where you spoke. Just about all our team members started implementing the things that you talked about. How do we keep this going?"

I gave him some suggestions on what to do at his weekly team meetings to reinforce the concepts covered in the original presentation. We decided to have a monthly phone call, and I told him that he would hear from someone on my team the first week of the month to set up a call. For him it was automatic. He didn't have to think about it. It was our responsibility. That's basically a subscription model. Like a monthly magazine that automatically shows up in a mailbox, he can count on our monthly conversation.

Of course, that's an external customer, but notice that the same idea can be applied very easily to internal customers. For instance, an IT person might say: "To make sure you feel totally comfortable using the new software and are successful with it, I'm going to suggest that we set up a series of phone calls. We could have a weekly 15-minute call so I can give you training, reinforcement and coaching until you feel like working on this platform is second nature to you. Would that make sense?"

Anytime you provide a resource when expected help or other resources come automatically, without anyone having to ask for it, you're reducing friction and delivering greater convenience.

START THE REVOLUTION!

These were just a few examples. I'm sure you can come up with many more. Use these ideas as a starting point. Start a Convenience Revolution of your own by thinking about how you can reduce friction for your customers and your colleagues on an individual level.

I'll close this book with the same question I asked you at the very beginning: *How easy is it to do business with you?*

Here's my promise. If you keep returning to that simple question, day after day, week after week, month after month – if you look closely and strategically at the honest answers that come back – then you really can join, and win, the Convenience Revolution. And I hope you do.

Acknowledgments

First and foremost, I want to thank you, the reader. This is my seventh book – twelve if you count the co-authored books. I wouldn't keep writing if you didn't keep reading, so a *BIG thank you* for your confidence in my work!

I find that writing a book isn't hard, but writing a *good* book is. Sometimes a little help makes a project like this so much better, and there were plenty of people who helped in bringing this book to fruition.

A big thank you to my friends at Cara Wordsmith, Ltd., who have worked with me on several books. They always make my ideas clearer, my stories and examples more relevant and the structure of the book easier to read. Basically, they make everything about the writing better. Mark Hunter, our college intern last summer, helped me research hundreds of companies to consider as examples in the book. Linda Read is an amazing editor and has been on the team for several books. Joan Dietrich gave the manuscript one last look before it went to the printer. (On a side note, Joan's mother, the late Audrey Dietrich, was on the editing team of my very first book, *Moments of Magic*, almost thirty years ago.) Jerry Dorris at AuthorSupport.com is a talented designer, and I appreciate his meticulous work on the interior of the book. And, there is my new publisher, Sound Wisdom. David Wildasin and the SW team are such a pleasure to work with!

Finally, Cindy Hyken, my wife, continues to be my biggest fan. In my last book, *Be Amazing or Go Home*, I thanked her for being amazing. She's still amazing – even more so. Thank you, Cindy, for all your love and support!

Potent Quote Sources

- Uber: https://www.thelocal.de/20140909/why-i-like-using-uber-taxi-app-germany

- The Ruhlin Group: https://www.forbes.com/sites/petertaylor/2016/06/20/how-to-expand-your-business-and-increase-sales-through-the-art-of-giftology/#4600144860c4.

- Ace Hardware: https://www.yelp.ie/biz/huffstutlers-ace-hardware-birmingham

- QuikTrip: https://www.youtube.com/watch?v=0-NoE2SCa38

- CLEAR: https://thepointsguy.com/guide/clear-expedited-airport-security/

- Google: http://allwomenstalk.com/8-reasons-why-i-love-google

- Panera Bread Company: http://uk.businessinsider.com/panera-bread-20-kiosk-ordering-system-2015-11?r=US&IR=T/#and-of-course-the-food-is-still-delicious-nothing-has-changed-here-steaming-hot-so-while-human-contact-may-have-decreased-at-panera-the-eating-experience-is-ultimately-the-same-11

- WalkMe: https://www.softwareadvice.co.ke/software/10398/walkme

- IKEA: https://www.inc.com/graham-winfrey/the-genius-design-elements-that-made-ikea-a-massive-success.html

- Salesforce: https://www.youtube.com/watch?v=VAb5tOuncKc

- Delta Airlines: https://www.yelp.ie/biz/delta-air-lines-kansas-city

- Starwood Hotels: http://www.stayntouch.com/blog/hotel-self-service-check-in/

- PayPal: https://www.reddit.com/r/paypal/comments/4tgusp/i_love_paypal/

- Square: https://www.fastcompany.com/1643271/square-brings-credit-card-swiping-mobile-masses-starting-today

- Geico Mobile: https://www.geico.com/web-and-mobile/mobile-apps/

- Domino's Pizza: http://natie.com/post/why-i-love-dominos-pizza/

- Walgreens: https://www.retaildive.com/ex/mobilecommercedaily/walgreens-leverages-consumer-first-mobile-strategy-to-drive-in-store-mobile-traffic

- NoWait: https://venturebeat.com/2015/10/25/why-i-insist-every-vc-and-employee-at-my-startup-first-train-as-a-restaurant-host/

- Netflix: https://www.emarketer.com/Article/ Convenience-Cost-Content-Power-Netflix-Uptake/1012730

- The New York Times: https://www.cjr.org/business_of_news/news-paywalls-new-york-times-wall-street-journal.php

- Spotify:https://www.wonderoftech.com/the-10-real-reasons-why-i-love-spotify/

- Dollar Shave Club: https://itunes.apple.com/us/app/dollar-shave-club/ id938309296?mt=8

- Blue Apron: http://simplytaralynn.com/2017/05/18/16-reasons-love-blue-apron/

- Microsoft Office: https://www.linkedin.com/pulse/ authentic-reasons-why-i-love-microsofts-office-365-moses-kemibaro/

- Kirkwood Audi: https://www.facebook.com/pg/AudiKirkwood/reviews/

- Monoprix: http://frenchgirlinseattle.com/shopping-au-monoprix/

- USPack: http://www.marketwired.com/press-release/uspack-logistics-completes-two-acquisitions-in-nationwide-expansion-2181825.htm

- Insomnia Cookies: https://spoonuniversity.com/lifestyle/insomnia-cookies

- Tom James: https://www.yelp.ie/biz/tom-james-clothiers-centennial

- 1-800-Flowers.com: https://www.mobilemarketer.com/ news/1-800-flowers-debuts-google-assistant-ordering/506559/

- Huntington Bank: https://wallethub.com/profile/ the-huntington-national-bank-13007162i/

- Enterprise Rent-A-Car: https://www.yelp.ie/biz/enterprise-rent-a-car-lemon-grove

- Walmart: https://www.qualitylogoproducts.com/blog/business-loyalty-walmart/

- Anytime Fitness: https://www.tripadvisor.ie/ShowUserReviews-g49367-d8027707-r274479854-Anytime_Fitness-Morehead_City_North_Carolina.html

- Starbucks: https://qz.com/334269/ what-starbucks-has-done-to-american-home-values/

- Moby Mart: http://www.wired.co.uk/article/moby-autonomous-shopping-store

- Matthew Dixon: https://www.amazon.com/Effortless-Experience-Conquering-Battleground-Customer/dp/1591845815/ref=sr_1_3?ie=UTF8&qid=15086855 55&sr=8-3&keywords=matthew+dixon

Index

ABOUT THE AUTHOR

Shep Hyken is the founder and Chief Amazement Officer at Shepard Presentations, where he helps companies build loyal relationships with their customers and employees. He is a customer service and experience expert, an award-winning keynote speaker, and a *New York Times* and *Wall Street Journal* bestselling author.

His articles have appeared in hundreds of publications. He is the author of *Moments of Magic, The Loyal Customer, The Cult of the Customer, The Amazement Revolution, Amaze Every Customer Every Time*, and *Be Amazing or Go Home*. His wide variety of clients range from smaller companies with less than 50 employees to corporate giants such as American Express, Anheuser-Busch, AT&T, Disney, Enterprise Rent-A-Car, General Motors, Great Clips, Greyhound, Häagen-Dazs, IBM, In-N-Out Burger, Lexus, Marriott, Merrill Lynch, Microsoft, Proctor & Gamble, Salesforce, Toyota and many more!

A prolific speaker well-known for his content-rich, entertaining and high-energy presentations, Hyken has been inducted into the National Speakers Hall of Fame for lifetime achievement in the speaking industry.

Learn more about Shep Hyken's speaking programs, customer service training programs and advisory services at www.Hyken.com.

Follow on Twitter: @Hyken
Like on Facebook: ShepHykenSpeaker
Connect on LinkedIn: www.Linkedin.com/in/ShepHyken
Join on Google +: www.gplus.to/ShepHyken
Watch on YouTube: www.ShepTV.com
Follow on Instagram: @ShepHyken